VEGAN CHEESE

ALSO BY JULES ARON

Zen and Tonic

VEGAN CHEESE
SIMPLE, DELICIOUS, PLANT-BASED RECIPES

By Jules Aron

THE COUNTRYMAN PRESS

A division of W. W. Norton & Company

Independent Publishers Since 1923

For information about permission to reproduce selections from this book,
write to Permissions, The Countryman Press, 500 Fifth Avenue, New York, NY 10110

For information about special discounts for bulk purchases, please contact
W. W. Norton Special Sales at specialsales@wwnorton.com or 800-233-4830

Manufacturing by Toppan Leefung
Book design by Nick Caruso Design
Production manager: Devon Zahn

The Countryman Press
www.countrymanpress.com

A division of W. W. Norton & Company, Inc.
500 Fifth Avenue, New York, NY 10110
www.wwnorton.com

978-1-58157-403-6

10 9 8 7 6 5 4 3 2 1

To Dolce—my loyal companion, my favorite travel buddy,
my dedicated kitchen assistant, and taste tester extraordinaire,
you will forever remain the dolce to my vita.

CONTENTS

VEGAN CHEESE

INTRODUCTION

BRIE, MOZZARELLA, CHEDDAR, GOAT, SWISS, GORGONZOLA, FETA . . .

Cheese, glorious cheese. The possibilities are endless, and the rich—and decadent—goodness is hard to resist. After all, what would a perfectly baked slice of pizza be without it? Or the extra hint of richness in your favorite sandwich? With its impossible-to-resist combination of fat, salt, and creaminess, it's hardly surprising that meals simply feel incomplete without the warm, gooey addition.

Since before recorded history, cheese has been one of the most beloved and sought-after foods in the world. Blocks, wheels, sprinkles, spreads, slices, and shreds. Hard cheeses and soft ones, pungent cheeses and mild ones. Today, Americans eat about 33 pounds of cheese a year, three times the rate of 1970. And yet with all this cheese consumption, it is estimated that a staggering 50 million Americans suffer from some degree of dairy intolerance or allergy. Even those of us without dairy-related discomforts are now looking for ways to opt out of the environmentally unsustainable, cruel, and unhealthy products available in the market today.

As we shift away from processed foods to real, clean ingredients, it's only natural that we would look for better dairy-free cheese alternatives as well.

Up until quite recently, casein-filled cheeselike shreds and overprocessed slices, often flavorless, strangely textured, and hard to digest, with unwelcome ingredients—such as vegetable glycerin, titanium dioxide, and my all-time favorite, "natural" flavors and colors—were the only dairy-free consumer cheese options.

Yet the increasing popularity of nut milks in recent years has changed the plant-based cheese landscape forever. Forward-thinking artisanal companies, such as Miyo-ko's Kitchen, Dr. Cow, and Vromage are now creating creamy and inventive nut-based offerings that will satisfy the harshest of cheese critics.

With little time and effort, you, too, can easily dazzle your friends, family, and guests by making your own rich and creamy varieties at home. Whether you're preparing an easy pasta dinner for the family, craving a cheesy snack, or planning an artisanal platter for the ultimate wine, beer, and cocktail pairing party, the following plant-based cheese recipes have you covered, no matter the occasion.

Versatile and fun, they can also make a tremendous contribution to your well-being. Made with nuts, seeds, beans, and veggies, these cheeses contribute iron, fiber, and naturally occurring phytochemicals to your diet. They are also naturally low in fat and saturated fat and are all cholesterol-free and significantly lower in sodium than dairy cheeses.

DAIRY VS. NONDAIRY CHEESE

The main difference between "real" cheese and vegan cheese is the consolidated protein, otherwise known as the curd. Dairy cheese goes through stages where the proteins physically bond to one another during the aging process. Vegan cheese, on the other hand, doesn't experience any modification in proteins and may not deliver the same complex flavors that come from coagulated, acidified, pasteurized, and aged milk. However, vegan cheeses can rival the taste and texture of many dairy varieties through the bacterial and aging process.

I've categorized the nondairy cheeses in this book primarily by texture and type: block and wheel for firm cheeses, soft and fresh for spreadable varieties, and sprinkles and sauces for quick and easy cheese fixes.

Several techniques are used in this book to produce a variety of cultured and uncultured cheeses. For cultured cheeses, "ripened" flavors are produced by brief periods of lacto-bacterial fermentation. For noncultured cheeses, sharper flavor profiles are created by introducing combinations of acids, such as vinegar or lemon juice. Both processes are simple and quite gratifying, although a little more patience is required for the cultured variety.

As you begin using this book, I invite you to look over the next few sections on pantry essentials and useful kitchen tools, to help you prepare for the recipes. There are also tips on how to prepare your own nut and seed milks, yogurt, and ferments. As you dog-ear the pages of the recipes you want to try, be sure to read the headnotes, tips, and variations offered, keeping in mind that some recipes call for components of other recipes, so you may have to prepare one ingredient beforehand. But it's always worth it!

At the end of each recipe, you'll find notes that cover everything from ingredient information to cooking suggestions, to possible variations on the recipes. My hope is that they'll complement and enhance your experience with the recipes.

For those who suffer from food allergies or sensitivities, I also make notations at the start of each recipe to indicate whether it is soy-free, nut-free, and/or seed-free. And because a nut or seed allergy should never stand between you and your vegan cheese, I am so very excited to note just how many vegetable cheese recipes I have listed.

Although there might be several unfamiliar ingredients and techniques in this book, don't get intimidated. The recipes are quite simple. The key to getting more comfortable is to start. Rather than shying away from an ingredient you've never heard of, embrace it. If there's a technique you haven't tried, just give it a whirl. You'll soon be amazed at these recipes' versatility and ease to prepare.

Most of all, I'm confident the recipes in this cookbook will have a positive impact on your health and well-being, and hopefully ignite your enthusiasm for simple, plant-based eating.

PREPPING YOUR KITCHEN

When it comes to prepping your space for making cheese, there are a few good habits to acquire right away. Here are some simple practices to get you started.

- Hot water is best to wash your equipment, utensils, and molds. Avoid using detergents that might leave a chemical residue. Use very hot water with a plain biodegradable soap, such as castile, instead.

- Make a solution of half white vinegar and half water and keep in a spray bottle to use as a general cleanser for your counter before beginning to work.

- Use clean, fresh kitchen towels when working with cheese.

- Avoid using plastic or wooden utensils that can harbor bacteria in small cracks. Choose stainless-steel utensils instead. Also choose glass and porcelain containers for storing the cheese mixtures.

- Store your kitchen tools within easy reach of your prep area, to increase your efficiency.

- Be prepared. Always review the recipe before beginning to make sure you have all you need at hand.

KITCHEN EQUIPMENT

Any craft has its tools, practices, and tricks of the trade. Stocking your kitchen with the appropriate equipment and ingredients will make cooking simple and efficient. To get you started on your cheese-making journey as quickly as possible, here is a comprehensive list of what you'll need (asterisked items are discussed in further detail). With these items on hand, you can make any recipe in this book.

Blender, high-speed*

Citrus juicer or reamer

Cheesecloth*

Glass bowls, various sizes*

Mason jars, wide-mouthed (pint- and quart-size, with a mesh lid)

Measuring cups, dry (various sizes)

Measuring cups, liquid (1- and 2-cup)

Measuring spoons

Molds, forms, and containers*

Nonstick saucepan (nontoxic, such as Ecopan)*

Nut milk bag*

Plastic wrap

Spatula, silicone*

Strainer, fine-mesh*

Thermometer*

Waxed paper

Whisk, silicone

BLENDER, HIGH-SPEED If you are going to buy just one kitchen appliance, hands down, a blender is it. High-powered blenders make quick work of nuts and can turn them into nut butters and nut milks within minutes. Unlike a food processor, which chops and grinds ingredients, high-speed blenders truly blend, creating creamy, smooth consistencies essential in nondairy cheese making.

CHEESECLOTH A woven gauzelike cotton cloth used primarily in cheese making. Cheesecloths can also be used in place of a nut bag for straining solids from nut milks. Look for the Butter Muslin or Grade 90# variety. The common cheesecloth is not as finely woven and four layers are usually required to efficiently strain plant milks and cheeses. You will need an 18-inch square piece of cheesecloth to work with.

GLASS BOWLS Staples of any kitchen, a variety of bowls is especially handy for our purposes. You'll need a set of glass bowls, in a variety of sizes, for both the fermentation process, and at least one large and deep enough so that when you place the strainer over it, it fits with room for the drip.

MOLDS, FORMS, AND CONTAINERS Professional cheese molds are wonderful but really quite unnecessary. Any food-safe container will work perfectly. Small bowls, ramekins, muffin pans, cookie cutters, and even silicone ice cube trays will work wonders.

NONSTICK SAUCEPAN A convenient cooking surface that prevents food from sticking while cooking. It is extremely invaluable when working with dairy- and plant-based milks and cheese mixes. Most, however, contain extremely toxic chemicals. Look for Ecopans. These ceramic pans use eco-friendly ingredients to produce a nonstick surface for easier nontoxic cooking.

NUT MILK BAG Made from ultrafine nylon mesh, they are effective tools for straining small particles of solids from nut, seed, and grain milks. Nut milks bags are also reusable.

SILICONE SPATULA This flexible, heat-resistant spatula makes it simple to get your mixtures out of blenders and bowls, especially when working with sticky, cheesy ingredients.

STRAINER, FINE-MESH Fine-mesh strainers have many uses in the kitchen. For our purposes, we'll use them to strain liquid out of our cheesy mixtures. Look for one that would comfortably fit over a medium bowl.

THERMOMETER Although not necessary, a thermometer is a handy tool while you are learning to read the temperature of the milk. Any food-safe, mercury-free thermometer will do.

YOUR VEGAN CHEESE PANTRY

Several indispensable ingredients are regularly used in the cheese recipes included in this book. Some may be very familiar while others may not be. Before attempting the recipes, it's helpful to understand what these ingredients are and why they are used. This list will make it simple to stock your pantry with all the cheese staples you'll need and will allow you to prepare the cheeses on short notice.

AGAR, also called agar-agar, is a plant-based gelatin substitute made of a tasteless seaweed derivative. It is used as a stabilizing and thickening agent. Agar is available in flake, stick, and powder form. The powdered form dissolves most easily in hot water and is easier to work with in our recipes. Something to note when cooking with agar is that it is not heat reversible, meaning that agar-based cheeses will not melt.

CARRAGEENAN is also a seaweed derivative that has been used as a thickening, stabilizing, and gelling agent for hundreds of years. Carrageenan comes in three forms, but for the purposes of cheese making, look for Kappa carrageenan. It can be purchased online from specialty food retailers listed in the resource page of this book (page 179). We will use it to make firm block and wheel cheeses.

CAULIFLOWER The spongy, anti-inflammatory, heart-healthy flowering vegetable we know as cauliflower is a good source of protein, phosphorous, and potassium. It is also one of our superstar cheese-making vegetables.

CHICKPEAS, also called garbanzo beans, are an excellent source of fiber, protein, and the mineral manganese that helps support bone development and wound healing. Best of all, the flavor and texture of the heart-healthy chickpea makes it another star in vegetable-based cheeses.

CHICKPEA MISO PASTE is a Japanese seasoning paste produced through the fermentation of chickpeas with salt and the fungus kojikin. I use chickpea miso for its mild savory taste. It contributes to the cheese's ripened flavor.

EXTRA-FIRM TOFU is made from soy milk that has been coagulated and pressed in a process not dissimilar from how cheese is made. The recipes in this book call for extra-firm tofu. Be sure to select an organic, non-genetically-modified (non-GMO) brand.

FILTERED OR SPRING WATER has been purified through filtration to remove chlorine and impurities. It is recommended in all recipes and is essential for producing live bacterial cultures that are used for fermenting plant-based milks, cream, and cheeses.

QUINOA This protein-rich grain keeps our red blood cells healthy and creates proper energy production in our cells. And it can be used to create the irresistible creamy texture in vegetable cheeses.

NUTRITIONAL YEAST, affectionately termed "nooch," is a nonactive form of yeast that has a cheesy, nutty flavor and is often used as a vegan cheese sprinkle. Rich in protein, minerals, and especially B vitamins, it is often used as a nutritional supplement. Nutritional yeast flakes can be found in most natural food stores or from online food retailers. Be sure to check the resource section at the end of this book.

NONDAIRY MILK There are many nondairy milks on the market. Look for fortified varieties and those using organic, non-GMO ingredients. Or better yet, make your own by following the recipes on pages 33–34.

NONDAIRY YOGURT Soy-, coconut-, and nut-based dairy-free yogurts are commercially available. If you would like to make your own, follow my homemade recipe on page 37.

NUTS AND SEEDS Rich in energy and protein, packed with antioxidants and omega-3 fatty acids, nuts and seeds also contain vitamin E, trace minerals, and fiber. A great number of the plant-based cheese recipes in this book are made with seeds and nuts.

ORGANIC REFINED COCONUT OIL Extracted from the flesh of the coconut, coconut oil is essential for thickening many of the cheese recipes in the book. Similar to dairy butter but without the cholesterol, organic refined coconut oil can be found in the natural section of most grocery stores.

PROBIOTICS are friendly bacteria often taken as a health supplement. Found mostly in capsule form, in the supplement section of your health food store, the powder is used as the starter for culturing cheeses, for taste and texture. Simply open probiotic capsules and empty the powder into a small bowl. A teaspoon is usually equivalent to six to eight capsules.

RAW APPLE CIDER VINEGAR This light, golden brown vinegar is made from organic and unpasteurized apple cider. Look for organic, unpasteurized apple cider vinegar that has the edible sediment known as "the mother."

REJUVELAC This nonalcoholic fermented liquid made from grain serves as a culturing agent for fermenting cheeses. It helps create the tangy, sharp and ripened quality in cultured cheeses.

SWEET POTATO provides vital minerals—such as iron, calcium, magnesium, manganese, and potassium—that are essential for enzyme, protein, and carbohydrate metabolism. The starchy tuber also helps create wonderfully creamy vegetable cheeses.

TAHINI This paste, made of sesame seeds, is nutty in flavor and is used in some plant-based cheeses to enhance flavor and texture.

TAPIOCA FLOUR This gluten-free flour (aka tapioca starch), made from cassava root, is an excellent thickening agent that produces a gooey, stretchy texture when heated in liquids. It is the thickener of choice in my cheese sauce, dip, and fondue recipes. Available in natural food stores or online retailers.

ZUCCHINI An outstanding source of manganese and vitamin C, the zucchini, also known as courgette, is technically a fruit. Its subtle taste and buttery white flesh make zucchini another superstar in the world of vegetable-based cheeses.

HERBS AND SPICES

Herbs and spices are used readily to boost flavor and add interest in most of the recipes in this book, but are also some of the healthiest foods as well. They raise the flavor profile of the homemade cheese itself and of whatever other ingredients it's being mixed and matched with. They can also be fun to experiment with when trying to switch up a dish. The herbs and spices used throughout the book include:

BASIL Antiaging, anti-inflammatory, eases arthritis pain

BLACK PEPPERCORNS Aids digestion, increases metabolism

CARDAMOM Promotes heart health, aids digestion

CAYENNE PEPPER Reduces inflammation, boosts metabolism

CHILI POWDER Regulates blood pressure, reduces pain

CILANTRO Soothes sore throat, speeds digestion

CINNAMON Helps control blood sugar, reduces bad cholesterol

DILL Helps control levels of blood cholesterol, antioxidant

GARLIC Protects against heart disease, antibacterial, antiviral

GINGER Aids digestion, soothes upset stomach, anti-inflammatory

MUSTARD Improves circulation, relieves congestion

OREGANO Antibacterial, antifungal, reduces inflammation

PARSLEY Calms nerves, antioxidant

ROSEMARY Improves digestion, enhances concentration

SEA SALT Offers trace minerals that have been processed out of table salt

THYME Reduces inflammation, controls blood pressure

TURMERIC Regulates hormones, boosts metabolism, anti-inflammatory

WASABI Improves circulation, boosts metabolism

NUTS AND SEEDS

Thanks to the prevalence of plant-based diets and a growing focus on health, nutrition-packed nuts and seeds are more popular than ever. Extremely versatile, they can be turned into milks, flours, and butters. They can also be made into cheeses, sauces, and spreads. Since a great number of the plant-based cheese recipes in this book are nut- or seed-based, let's go through some basics.

We will be using a variety of nuts and seeds that not only add distinct taste variations, but also affect the texture of nondairy cheeses. Almonds make clean-tasting cheeses; macadamias, lovely creamy varieties that develop good firm texture; while cashews produce smooth, easy-to-flavor cheeses with softer textures. Seeds, especially sunflower, hemp, and pumpkin, add an almost smoky taste to cheeses, and cheeses made with pine nuts are very rich and distinctive. Follow the recipes in this book to get a sense of the variations, then have fun experimenting on your own.

SUBSTITUTING NUTS AND SEEDS

Many of the nuts and seeds used in the recipes are interchangeable. Nuts and seeds with similar texture can be easily swapped for personal preference or convenience. Note, however, that these changes may alter the flavor profile of the recipe.

The nut- and seed-based cheese recipes in the book all call for nuts and seeds in their raw form to avoid the denaturing of nutrients and the breakdown of fats that could make them more vulnerable to oxidation when exposed to high temperatures. They do, however, require soaking.

Always begin by soaking your nuts and seeds, following the recommended times in the handy table on page 29. Make sure to rinse and drain them properly. Allot enough time for soaking before beginning a recipe or prepare to have soaked nuts ready in the

refrigerator. Soaked and drained nuts will keep, refrigerated, for five days; soaked and drained seeds will keep for three days.

When blending soaked nuts and/or seeds in your high-speed blender, make sure to scrape down the sides of the blender bowl to ensure a smooth and creamy texture. Always strain the cheese mixture through a cheesecloth-lined strainer to eliminate any excess moisture.

When working with almonds, it is essential that they be skinless, to ensure the creamy texture necessary for cheese making. Blanching your own almonds is a simple process and is much more cost effective than buying them blanched.

To blanch almonds, bring a small pot of water to a boil. Place your raw almonds in the boiling water and let them boil for exactly one minute. Drain the almonds immediately in a colander and rinse them with cold water. Blot the almonds dry. Carefully squeeze the almonds with your fingers to loosen the skin. You now have blanched almonds.

Most nuts and seeds are common and widely available. You can find online resources for quality bulk nuts and seeds if your natural food store doesn't carry them. Remember that all the recipes in this book call for raw nuts and seeds.

STORING: Store raw nuts and seeds in sealable containers, such as mason jars, and keep in the refrigerator or freezer for maximum shelf life.

SOAKING: Soaking nuts and seeds is essential to soften them before processing, which makes the puree creamier and the puree process easier and quicker. It is especially important when the water content in the recipe is low. Presoaking is less vital when larger amounts of water is used for processing.

To soak nuts and seeds, place in a mason jar, fill with twice as much water by volume, screw the lid closed and leave for the specified time at room temperature. Drain the nuts or seeds and rinse thoroughly. Soaked and drained nuts will keep, refrigerated, for five days; soaked and drained seeds will keep for three days.

NUTS AND SEEDS		FLAVOR AND TEXTURE	SOAKING TIME
NUTS	Almonds	Creamy and mild	8 to 12 hours
	Brazil nuts	Rich and creamy	6 hours
	Cashews	Rich and creamy	6 hours
	Hazelnuts	Nutty and rich	8 to 12 hours
	Macadamias	Thick and rich	6 hours
	Pecans	Hearty and nutty	8 hours
	Pine nuts	Rich and earthy	1 hour
	Pistachios	Creamy and rich	8 hours
	Walnuts	Nutty and hearty	8 hours
SEEDS	Chia	Neutral	none
	Flax	Smooth and nutty	1 hour
	Hemp	Mild, thick, and creamy	none
	Pumpkin	Strong flavored	8 hours
	Sesame	Rich and nutty	6 hours
	Sunflower	Nutty and slightly bitter	8 hours

Nuts are rich in protein, vitamins, minerals, and essential unsaturated and monounsaturated fats. Seeds are also high in protein, B vitamins, minerals, essential unsaturated and monounsaturated fats, and dietary fibers.

Recipes in this section

Nut/Seed Milk Master Recipe • Coconut Milk
Homemade Yogurt • Do-It-Yourself Rejuvelac

PANTRY STAPLES

NUT AND SEED MILKS ARE EASY TO MAKE AT HOME, AND MAKE A PER-
fect base for these cheese recipes. Simply blended with water, many types of nuts and
seeds transform into a deliciously creamy milk alternative. Almond milk, in particular,
has become the most popular alternative to dairy and soy milk. It contains no saturated fats or cholesterol, and supplies 25 percent of our daily vitamin D needs as well as
half of our daily vitamin E requirements.

New varieties of nut and seed milks are becoming increasingly available in stores;
however, making them at home offers its advantages: a fresh, clean product with no
added salts, sugars, or preservatives and one that is more economical as well. If you are
buying your product at the store, look for unsweetened and organic varieties.

A note about soy: Soy milk and soy products are a great source of protein and work
very well in cheese recipes. However, they are also some of the most genetically modi-
fied foods on the market today. I have, for this reason, significantly limited the number
of recipes that call for soy. If you prefer to use soy milk in the recipes, choose one that
is unflavored and organic.

NUT/SEED MILK MASTER RECIPE

NUT/SEED	QUANTITY	WATER
Almonds	1 cup	3 cups
Brazil nuts	1 cup	3 cups
Cashews	1 cup	3 cups
Macadamias	1 cup	3 cups
Hazelnuts	1 cup	2 cups
Flaxseeds	¼ cup	3 cups
Sunflower seeds	1 cup	3 cups
Hemp seeds	½ cup	4 cups

This basic recipe works with most nuts or seeds. Store for up to three to five days in the refrigerator. If the milk separates, shake or blend again before using.

*Makes 2 to 4 cups
nut or seed milk*

Soy-Free

VARIATIONS For creams, reduce the water by half; for skim milks, add additional water.

TRICK OF THE TRADE Besides yielding a creamier milk, soaking releases enzyme inhibitors that make the nuts or seeds easier to digest.

Soak the nuts or seeds following the appropriate soaking times in the table on page 29. Strain the soaked nuts or seeds and rinse well. Place them in your blender, add the measured water (see chart above), and process until smooth. Use a fine-mesh strainer, cheesecloth, or nut milk bag to strain out any particles.

TASTY TWEAKS Customize the flavor of nut and seed milks with these tasty add-ins:

Vanilla Milk—Add 1 tablespoon of pure vanilla extract and blend with one or two pitted dates or your preferred natural sweetener.

Chocolate Milk—Add 1 tablespoon of raw cacao and sweeten with organic raw agave or pure maple syrup. Use hazelnuts for an extra-special Nutella-like milk!

Strawberry Rose Milk—Blend in 1 cup of fresh or frozen strawberries and add 2 teaspoons of pure rose water.

Carrot Cake Milk—Blend in two chopped medium carrots, 1 teaspoon of pure vanilla extract, 1½ teaspoons of ground cinnamon, and ¼ teaspoon of ground cardamom. Sweeten to taste.

Chai Milk—Add ½ teaspoon of ground cardamom, ¼ teaspoon of ground cinnamon, two peppercorns, and three thin slivers of ginger. Sweeten with dates or pure maple syrup to taste.

Matcha Milk—Add 1½ teaspoons of matcha green tea powder; sweeten to taste.

COCONUT MILK

———*//*———

Making your own coconut milk is a pure delight. If you have access to young coconuts, I encourage you to try your hand at this lovely milk alternative. Nothing like the overly processed and sweetened canned variety, homemade coconut milk is very low in calories and has tremendous health benefits.

Makes 2 to 3 cups coconut milk

Nut-Free / Soy-Free

1 to 2 young Thai coconuts (use both meat and water)

Remove all the coconut meat and water from the shell. Rinse and place the coconut meat in a blender, add the coconut water, and process until smooth. Strain the mixture to remove any small shell particles.

TRICK OF THE TRADE Hate to throw away the blended pulp used for milk? Add it to smoothies to boost protein and fiber or turn into a meal or flour, for use in cookies, crusts, and crackers.

HOW TO MAKE NUT FLOUR

Store-bought coconut and almond flour can be quite pricey. Making your own from the strained solids of your nut milks, however, is quite simple. Pour the strained-out solids onto a parchment-lined baking sheet and bake at 250°F for 2 to 3 hours. Place in a blender and process into a flour. The flour will keep refrigerated for up to 5 days.

2 cups cashews, soaked

4 cups water, filtered

2 teaspoons probiotic powder

HOMEMADE YOGURT

—————//—————

Nondairy yogurt is packed with fiber, calcium, protein, and probiotics— live cultures of beneficial bacteria, to promote digestive health and stimulate your immune system. While there are a few commercial vegan yogurts on the market today, making your own is fun and easy, and the best way to avoid added sugars and fillers. Having some on hand will be useful for a few of the cheese recipes in this book.

Makes about 4 cups

PREP AND COOK TIME
under 30 minutes

WAIT TIME
8 to 12 hours

Seed-Free / Soy-Free

Place the nuts and water in a blender and process until smooth. Pour the nut milk into a medium saucepan and heat over medium-low heat until it reaches 100°F. If the mixture is too hot, it may destroy the culture. Remove from the heat and whisk in the probiotic powder.

Pour the yogurt into a large jar, wrap in a kitchen towel, and leave in a warm place to culture for 8 to 12 hours or overnight. The yogurt will thicken and will start to taste and smell slightly tangy. Refrigerate until ready to use (up to 2 weeks).

TRICK OF THE TRADE You may need to experiment with the length of time that the yogurt cultures and with the amount of probiotic you use. Everyone has different taste preferences and experimenting will allow you to customize your yogurt to your taste.

VARIATIONS AND SUBSTITUTIONS You can substitute either a vegan yogurt starter or 2 tablespoons of store-bought nondairy, soy-free yogurt for the probiotics.

1 cup wheat berries or uncooked quinoa

12 cups water, filtered, plus extra for rinsing

DO-IT-YOURSELF
REJUVELAC

Rejuvelac is a nonalcoholic fermented liquid made from sprouted grains. It is a simple and inexpensive way to make probiotic rich in lactobacilli, nutrients, and enzymes. We will use it often as a culturing agent for our nut and seed milks and nondairy cheeses.

Makes 6 cups

PREP AND COOK TIME
*24 hours for quinoa or
48 hours for wheat berries*

WAIT TIME
2 to 3 days

Nut-Free / Seed-Free / Soy-Free

Divide the wheat berries between two quart-size wide-mouth mason jars and cover each with 3 cups filtered water. Secure the tops with cheesecloth or use a mesh lid and let sit overnight, then drain. Rinse and drain the grains twice a day, laying the jar on its side, until you see sprouts (about 48 hours for the wheat berries or 24 hours for quinoa).

Once the grain has sprouted, rinse, drain, and refill each jar with 3 cups filtered water. Cover with a lid and leave at room temperature, out of direct sunlight, for 2 to 3 days, until the water is cloudy and bubbly.

Strain out the seeds and refrigerate the lactic acid–rich liquid. The rejuvelac will keep, refrigerated, for 3 to 4 weeks.

TRICK OF THE TRADE Do not use tap water as it may contain traces of chlorine, which will prevent fermentation.

You are now ready to create lusciously creamy, ultra-flavorful nondairy slices and spreads. As discussed in the introduction, there are many different kinds of methods for preparing vegan cheeses. Before beginning, make sure to read through the recipes first. Some of the cheese basics do take some time, mostly for setting, so it's good to plan ahead.

SPREADS, SAUCES, AND SPRINKLES

QUICK, EASY, AND CONVENIENT, THE CHEESE RECIPES IN THIS FIRST section require no waiting time. Whether it's a cheesy sprinkle or sauce you want, this section has got you covered—so you can get it covered with lots of cheesy goodness.

SWEET SPREAD

This enchanting simple spread, sweetened with dried currants and orange zest, is remarkably quick and easy to make and is perfect to have on hand for brunches at home or as a sweet snack.

Makes 8 to 10 ounces

PREP AND COOK TIME
15 minutes

WAIT TIME
ready immediately

Seed-Free / Soy-Free

1 cup raw cashews, soaked, rinsed, and drained (see page 28)

2 to 3 tablespoons water, filtered

2 tablespoons fresh lemon juice

2 tablespoons raw organic agave syrup

1 tablespoon orange zest

2 tablespoons dried currants, soaked

Place the cashews, water, lemon juice, and agave in a blender and process until smooth. Transfer the mixture to a bowl and stir in the orange zest and currants. Store, refrigerated, in a sealed jar; will keep for 5 to 7 days.

CLASSIC FONDUE

———— // ————

This simple and elegant fondue makes terrific fare for intimate gatherings and romantic dinners. Serve with warm chunks of French bread or chips or an assortment of roasted, steamed, or raw vegetables.

Makes about 4 cups

PREP AND COOK TIME
under 40 minutes

WAIT TIME
ready immediately

Soy-Free / Seed-Free

CHEESE

2 cups raw cashews, soaked, rinsed, and drained
(see page 28)

½ cup rejuvelac (see page 38)

¼ cup organic refined coconut oil, melted

2 tablespoons nutritional yeast

2 tablespoons chickpea miso paste

1 teaspoon sea salt

FONDUE

1 cup dry white wine

3 tablespoons tapioca flour

2 tablespoons water, filtered

To make the cheese, process the cheese ingredients in a blender until smooth and creamy.

To make the fondue, pour the wine into a saucepan, bring to a boil, add the cheese mixture, and whisk to combine. Heat until very hot.

Meanwhile, in a small bowl, dissolve the tapioca flour in the water, then stir into the cheese mixture, whisking well. Cook until the mixture is thick, stretchy, and shiny. Serve in a fondue dish.

TRICK OF THE TRADE If you prefer a thinner cheese sauce, add more wine or water.

EASY CHEESY OAT AND BEAN SAUCE

One 15-ounce can cannellini beans or other white beans

1 cup rolled oats

2 tablespoons tapioca flour

2 tablespoons nutritional yeast

1 tablespoon minced garlic

1 tablespoon paprika

1 teaspoon sea salt

1½ cups water, filtered

This quick oat and cannellini bean cheese sauce is a wonder to have on hand. Creamy and velvety, with a subtle tang, it makes a delicious topping. Try it on your favorite noodles or pizza or as a tasty, stand-alone dip.

Makes 2 to 3 cups

PREP AND COOK TIME
under 30 minutes

WAIT TIME
ready immediately

Nut-Free / Seed-Free / Soy-Free

Drain and rinse the beans to remove the salt. Place the beans in a blender and process by pulsing a few times, then add and process the rest of the ingredients, except the water. Add the water slowly, continuing to process, until a smooth and creamy texture is achieved. Store, refrigerated, in a sealed jar; will keep for 5 to 7 days.

SPICY QUESO SAUCE WITH QUINOA, SWEET POTATO, AND CORN

———— // ————

This delicately balanced cheese sauce is made with quinoa, sweet potatoes, and corn for a lovely spicy treat. Perfect as a vegetable dip or as a topping for your steamed veggies and baked potatoes.

Makes 2 to 3 cups

PREP AND COOK TIME
under 30 minutes

WAIT TIME
ready immediately

Nut-Free / Seed-Free / Soy-Free

½ cup uncooked quinoa

1 cup peeled and boiled sweet potato

½ cup cooked or canned corn

1½ cups nondairy, soy-free milk

2 tablespoons ground flaxseeds

1 teaspoon sea salt

1 tablespoon chipotle sauce (or flavor of choice)

Cook the quinoa. Transfer to a blender. Add the remaining ingredients and process until a smooth consistency is achieved. Store, refrigerated, in a sealed jar; will keep for 5 to 7 days.

TRICK OF THE TRADE Quinoa is a quick-cooking grain that packs a nutritional punch. It is a complete source of protein, high in calcium and iron. Before cooking, take the time to rinse quinoa for a few minutes to remove the saponin, its natural pesticide.

Flaxseeds are tiny brown seeds that are an excellent source of omega-3 fatty acids and fiber. They add a pleasant mild nutty flavor to cheese recipes.

HARISSA HEMP SPREAD

———— // ————

This Moroccan-spiced nut-free spread will be your new go-to favorite. Not only is it high in omega-3 fatty acids, it is quick and easy to prepare.
Use it as a dip or to add that extra flair to your sandwiches.

Makes about 1 cup

PREP AND COOK TIME
under 15 minutes

WAIT TIME
ready immediately

Nut-Free / Soy-Free

1 cup raw hemp hearts (hulled hemp seeds)

1 garlic clove

3 tablespoons fresh lemon juice

3 tablespoons hemp milk

1 tablespoon chopped fresh parsley

½ to 1 teaspoon harissa paste

½ teaspoon sea salt

Place all the ingredients in a blender and process to a smooth, creamy consistency. Store, refrigerated, in a sealed jar; will keep for up to 1 week.

Harissa is a spicy and aromatic blend of hot chile peppers, tomatoes, garlic, olive oil, and such spices as cumin, coriander, caraway, mint, plus sometimes rose petals. Even if you love spicy food, harissa packs quite a punch. A little goes a long way.

CHEESY CHIA SAUCE

———//———

This luscious golden cheese sauce is thick and creamy, perfect for dipping. Serve with an assortment of crisps and veggies for ultimate snacking, or pour over your favorite noodles to elevate your mac and cheese experience.

Makes about 1 cup

PREP AND COOK TIME
under 15 minutes

WAIT TIME
ready immediately

Nut-Free / Soy-Free

½ cup raw hemp hearts (hulled hemp seeds)

2 tablespoons chia seeds

1 orange bell pepper, chopped

¼ cup nutritional yeast

1 teaspoon Dijon mustard

1 tablespoon chickpea miso paste

¼ teaspoon ground turmeric

¼ teaspoon sea salt

¼ teaspoon cayenne pepper

¼ cup hemp milk

Place all the ingredients in a blender and process to a thick and creamy texture. Store, refrigerated, in a sealed container; will keep for up to 1 week.

TRICK OF THE TRADE For a thinner sauce, just dilute with water or additional hemp milk.

VEGGIE NACHO DIP

———— // ————

Who would have thought it possible? This supremely creamy, spicy powerhouse of vegetables tastes like a real thick cheese sauce! Surprise all of your friends with this beautiful dip and see whether they can tell your secret.

Makes about 3 cups

PREP AND COOK TIME
under 30 minutes

WAIT TIME
ready immediately

Nut-Free / Seed-Free / Soy-Free

1 cup boiled cauliflower florets

1 cup boiled chopped carrot

½ cup diced tomato

½ red onion, diced

2 garlic cloves

1 jalapeño pepper, diced

1 teaspoon salt

1 teaspoon ground cumin

1 teaspoon ground turmeric

2 tablespoons nutritional yeast

¼ cup extra-virgin olive oil

½ cup tomato juice

Place all the ingredients in a blender and process until smooth. Store, refrigerated, in a sealed container; will keep for up to 1 week.

Turmeric, the bright, warm, peppery spice best known as a main ingredient used in curry, also gives ballpark mustard its bright yellow color. It is a powerful anti-inflammatory that has been used for centuries to treat wounds, infections, and other health problems.

BRAZIL NUT PECORINO

———— // ————

The perfect sprinkle for your favorite Italian dishes, this delightful cheesy topping is reminiscent of the classic Italian pecorino, made subtlety sharp here with tangy garlic.

Makes about 1 cup

PREP AND COOK TIME
under 15 minutes

WAIT TIME
ready immediately

Seed-Free / Soy-Free

1 cup raw, unsoaked Brazil nuts

¼ cup nutritional yeast

1 teaspoon sea salt

½ teaspoon garlic powder

Place all the ingredients in a blender and pulse until the mixture becomes mealy. Store, refrigerated, in a sealed jar; will keep for 3 to 4 weeks.

Affectionately termed "nooch," **nutritional yeast** is a flaky flavor enhancer that rivals salt and garlic thanks to its uniquely nutty, cheesy, creamy taste. This nutritional supplement made of inactive pasteurized yeast is an excellent source of complete protein and vitamins, especially the B-complex vitamins.

Pecorino
{BRASIL}

Parmesan
{SEEDS}

Parmesan
{WALNUT}

WALNUT PARMESAN

———————//———————

This simple three-ingredient
nut cheese is perfect on top
of pastas, pizza, and
anywhere else you'd like
a sprinkle of cheesy goodness.

Makes about 1 cup

PREP AND COOK TIME
under 15 minutes

WAIT TIME
ready immediately

Seed-Free / Soy-Free

1 cup raw, unsoaked walnuts

¼ cup nutritional yeast

½ teaspoon sea salt

Place all the ingredients in a blender and pulse until
the mixture becomes mealy. Store, refrigerated, in a
sealed jar; will keep for 3 to 4 weeks.

TRIPLE-SEED ROMANO

A seed alternative to the nutty Parmesan sprinkles.

Makes about 2 cups

PREP AND COOK TIME
under 15 minutes

WAIT TIME
ready immediately

Nut-Free / Soy-Free

1 cup raw, unsoaked sunflower seeds

1 cup raw, unsoaked pumpkin seeds

½ cup raw, unsoaked sesame seeds

1 tablespoon sea salt

1 tablespoon ground turmeric

2 tablespoons fresh lemon juice

Place all the ingredients in a blender and pulse until the mixture becomes mealy. Store, refrigerated, in a sealed jar; will keep for 3 to 4 weeks.

Agar Technique

Zucchini Cheese • Zucchini Hemp Seed Cheese • "Open Sesame" Cheese
Smoked Vegetable Cheese • American Slices • Cauliflower Jack • Sun Wheel
Swiss Cheese • Jalapeño Jack • Apple-Smoked Gouda • Smoked Chipotle
Chai-Spiced Cheese • Mediterranean Feta

Agar and Tapioca Technique

Sriracha Vegetable Cheese • Arugula Pesto Cheese
Provolone • French-Style Brie • Dark Chocolate Brie

Carrageenan and Tapioca Technique

Golden Cheddar • Mozzarella • Dill Havarti • Camembert

BLOCK AND WHEEL CHEESES

FOR FANS OF HARD CHEESE VARIETIES, THE FOLLOWING NONDAIRY block and wheel cheeses resemble their dairy counterparts in texture and flavor. They are also some of the faster cheeses you can create. Three different techniques are used in this category: agar, followed by agar and tapioca, and finally carrageenan and tapioca. The last two techniques are especially exciting because they make cheeses that melt beautifully.

You will need a glass or ceramic container that can hold up to 2 to 3 cups of liquid. This container will serve as your cheese form, so be mindful when choosing its shape. Although the wait time listed is two to four hours, keep in mind that this is the minimum amount of time recommended for the cheese to form and set. If you allow your cheese to chill overnight, your patience will be rewarded with a firmer, sharper cheese.

AGAR TECHNIQUE

Agar (aka agar-agar) is a colorless gelling agent made from seaweed, often used as a substitute for gelatin in vegan recipes. Agar is a good source of calcium and iron and is very high in fiber. It is known for its abilities to aid in digestion and to reduce inflammation.

The secret to success when using agar is to let it soak for five minutes in cold water to help dissolve it, then simmer the flakes in plenty of liquid for about eight minutes, or until all the bits have dissolved. Once cold, undissolved agar flakes turn grainy, so be sure the agar is dissolved completely before adding the mixture to the blender.

ZUCCHINI CHEESE

———//———

Nut and seed allergy sufferers, rejoice! This is a vegetable-based cheese just for you. Once you have mastered the basic technique, you can add your favorite herbs and spices to create your own flavor combinations.

Makes an approximately ½-pound block

PREP AND COOK TIME
under 30 minutes

WAIT TIME
2 to 4 hours

Nut-Free / Seed-Free / Soy-Free

CHEESE

1 cup peeled, sliced zucchini

1 tablespoon extra-virgin olive oil

1 tablespoon fresh lemon juice

1 tablespoon nutritional yeast

½ teaspoon sea salt

AGAR GEL

¼ cup cold water, filtered

¾ teaspoon agar powder

Steam the zucchini for 5 minutes. Drain and discard the water. Transfer the zucchini to a blender and add the olive oil, lemon juice, nutritional yeast, and salt. Blend until smooth.

To make the agar gel, whisk the cold water and the agar together in a saucepan. Let it soak for 5 minutes then bring to a boil. Lower the heat and simmer, whisking often, for 5 to 8 minutes, to activate the agar.

Once the agar mixture is ready, quickly transfer it to the cheese mixture in the blender and process until it becomes homogenous. Pour the mixture into a container and cover. Refrigerate until set, at least 2 to 4 hours.

Wrap the cheese in waxed paper and store in a sealed container. Will keep, refrigerated, for 5 to 7 days.

VARIATIONS AND SUBSTITUTIONS Once you've mastered the recipe, consider adding fresh herbs, your favorite hot sauce, smoked spices, or even olives and sun-dried tomatoes to the cheese ingredients.

ZUCCHINI HEMP SEED CHEESE

———— // ————

Light and nutritious,
this lovely seed cheese makes
a wonderful snack.
It is easily sliceable and can
be shredded with a light
touch to sprinkle over salads
and baked potatoes.

*Makes an approximately
1-pound block*

PREP AND COOK TIME
under 30 minutes

WAIT TIME
2 to 4 hours

Nut-Free / Soy-Free

CHEESE

½ cup raw hemp hearts (hulled hump seeds)

2 medium zucchini, peeled

1 cup hemp milk

¼ cup raw apple cider vinegar

½ cup raw pumpkin seeds, soaked

1 teaspoon sea salt

1 teaspoon minced garlic

¼ teaspoon ground turmeric

¼ cup nutritional yeast

AGAR GEL

1 cup cold water, filtered

2 tablespoons agar powder

Rinse the hemp hearts. Place them and all the other cheese ingredients in a blender and process until smooth. Leave the cheese mixture in the blender.

To make the agar gel, whisk the cold water and the agar together in a saucepan. Let it soak for 5 minutes then bring to a boil. Lower the heat and simmer, whisking often, for 5 to 8 minutes, to activate the agar.

Once the agar mixture is ready, quickly transfer it to the cheese mixture in the blender and process until it becomes homogenous. Pour the mixture into a container and cover. Refrigerate until firm and set, at least 2 to 4 hours.

Wrap the cheese in waxed paper and store in a sealed container. Will keep, refrigerated, for 5 to 7 days.

Hemp seeds are one of the most digestible and concentrated sources of complete protein, amino acids, and essential omega-3 fatty acids found in nature.

"OPEN SESAME" CHEESE

———— // ————

A simple, sliceable seed cheese made from unhulled sesame seeds. Nutty and satisfying, it delights with its smoky finish. A perfect snacking cheese to enjoy with crackers and a cold beer.

Makes 1 round (about 8 ounces)

PREP AND COOK TIME:
under 30 minutes

WAIT TIME
2 to 4 hours

Nut-Free / Soy-Free

CHEESE

½ cup raw, unhulled sesame seeds

1 tablespoon nutritional yeast

½ teaspoon sea salt

1 tablespoon raw apple cider vinegar

½ teaspoon paprika

2 tablespoons minced onion

1 teaspoon minced garlic

AGAR GEL

1 cup cold water, filtered

1 tablespoon agar powder

Grind the sesame seeds, nutritional yeast, and salt in a blender until a flour forms. Add the vinegar, paprika, onion, and garlic. Leave the cheese mixture in the blender.

To make the agar gel, whisk the cold water and the agar together in a saucepan. Let it soak for 5 minutes then bring to a boil. Lower the heat and simmer, whisking often, for 5 to 8 minutes, to activate the agar.

Once the agar mixture is ready, quickly transfer it to the cheese mixture in the blender and process until it becomes homogenous. Pour the mixture into a container and cover. Refrigerate until firm and set, at least 2 to 4 hours.

Wrap the cheese in waxed paper and store in a sealed container. Will keep, refrigerated, for 1 to 2 weeks.

Sesame seeds are embedded in a seed coat, or hull. Unhulled seeds are a good source of insoluble fiber, calcium, and iron and are also a significant source of B vitamins, particularly thiamine, vitamin B_6, niacin, and folate. Whole sesame seeds add a nutty, smoky complexity. If you prefer a more neutral flavor, you can easily substitute hulled seeds.

SMOKED VEGETABLE CHEESE

———————

This creamy-textured cheese has a sweet smokiness reminiscent of red peppers and sunshine. It easily slices and grates and has no nuts or soy-based ingredients, making it a great option for most individuals with food allergies.

Makes an approximately 1½-pound block

PREP AND COOK TIME
under 30 minutes

WAIT TIME
2 to 4 hours

Nut-Free / Seed-Free / Soy-Free

CHEESE

2 cups water, filtered

1 cup rolled oats

1 cup peeled, chopped, and boiled sweet potato

1 whole roasted red pepper

½ cup nutritional yeast

1 tablespoon smoked paprika

1 tablespoon sea salt

1 teaspoon onion powder

1 teaspoon garlic powder

2 tablespoons fresh lemon juice

AGAR GEL

1⅓ cups cold water, filtered

2 tablespoons agar powder

Place all the cheese ingredients in a blender. Process until smooth. Leave the cheese mixture in the blender.

To make the agar gel, whisk the cold water and the agar together in a saucepan. Let it soak for 5 minutes then bring to a boil. Lower the heat and simmer, whisking often, for 5 to 8 minutes, to activate the agar.

Once the agar mixture is ready, quickly transfer it to the cheese mixture in the blender and process until it becomes homogenous. Pour the mixture into a container and cover. Refrigerate until set, at least 2 to 4 hours.

Wrap the cheese in waxed paper and store in a sealed container. Will keep, refrigerated, for 5 to 7 days.

TRICK OF THE TRADE Noncultured cheeses can keep refrigerated up to 3 weeks. Shelf life can be influenced by several factors including moisture content, temperature, acid, salt, and bacteria. Because of the high moisture content of vegetable cheeses, their shelf life is reduced to 5 to 7 days.

AMERICAN SLICES

———— // ————

The same classic American cheese taste you grew up with: mild, firm, and satisfying. This creamy, golden-hued cheese is perfect sliced on sandwiches and crackers.

Makes an approximately 1-pound block

PREP AND COOK TIME
under 30 minutes

WAIT TIME
2 to 4 hours

Seed-Free / Soy-Free

CHEESE

1 cup raw cashews, soaked, drained, and rinsed (see page 28)

¼ cup fresh lemon juice

¼ cup water, filtered

1 large red bell pepper, chopped

⅓ cup nutritional yeast

2 tablespoons chopped red onion

2 garlic cloves, chopped

1 teaspoon yellow mustard

1 teaspoon sea salt

AGAR GEL

½ cup cold water, filtered

4 teaspoons agar powder

Place all the cheese ingredients in a blender. Process until smooth and creamy. Leave the cheese mixture in the blender.

To make the agar gel, whisk the cold water and the agar together in a saucepan. Let it soak for 5 minutes then bring to a boil. Lower the heat and simmer, whisking often, for 5 to 8 minutes, to activate the agar.

Once the agar mixture is ready, quickly transfer it to the cheese mixture in the blender and process until it becomes homogenous. Pour the mixture into a container and cover. Refrigerate until firm and set, at least 2 to 4 hours.

Wrap the cheese in waxed paper and store in a sealed container. Will keep, refrigerated, for 1 to 2 weeks.

TRICK OF THE TRADE Soaking the cashews in water for 4 to 8 hours makes the puree creamier and easier to process. It is required in recipes with low water content, such as cheeses.

CAULIFLOWER JACK

2 cups cauliflower florets

4 tablespoons vegan gelatin

3 tablespoons organic refined coconut oil, melted

1 tablespoon fresh lime juice

1 teaspoon sea salt

2 tablespoons nutritional yeast

1 teaspoon onion powder

1 teaspoon garlic powder

½ cup chopped fresh chives

This delicate vegetable cheese is a lovely mild white cheese reminiscent of the popular Monterey Jack. It melts beautifully and adapts easily to all your favorite recipes.

Makes an approximately 1-pound block

PREP AND COOK TIME
under 30 minutes

WAIT TIME
4 hours

Nut-Free / Seed-Free / Soy-Free

Steam the cauliflower until tender. Reserve ½ cup of the boiled water from the steamer pot to dissolve the gelatin.

In a bowl, hydrate the gelatin by sprinkling a little cold water over it to make it bloom. Add the reserved cauliflower water and whisk to combine.

In a blender, process the cauliflower, coconut oil, lime juice, sea salt, nutritional yeast, onion powder, and garlic powder until smooth. Transfer the gelatin mixture to the blender and add the chives. Blend to combine. Pour the cheese mixture in a container and cover. Refrigerate for 4 hours, until it firms and sets.

Store, refrigerated, in a sealed container; will keep for 5 to 7 days.

Regular gelatin is made of animal by-products, so be sure to choose a vegan gelatin, or follow the instructions for using agar instead. Check the resources at the end of the book for suppliers.

SUN WHEEL

––––//––––

This firm, nut-free seed cheese is perfect for everyday enjoyment. You can cube and skewer with toothpicks for hors d'oeuvres or slice and layer in sandwiches.

Makes an approximately 1-pound block

PREP AND COOK TIME
under 30 minutes

WAIT TIME
2 to 4 hours

Nut-Free / Soy-Free

Chickpea miso paste is a Japanese seasoning produced by the fermentation of chickpeas with salt and the fungus kojikin. The paste is used as a culturing and flavoring ingredient in some of the cheese recipes to give a ripened cheese flavor.

CHEESE

1 cup raw sunflower seeds, soaked, rinsed, and drained (see page 28)

1 cup raw pumpkin seeds, soaked, rinsed, and drained (see page 28)

1 cup water, filtered

½ cup nutritional yeast

½ cup fresh lemon juice

1 tablespoon chickpea miso paste

2 teaspoons sea salt

1 teaspoon onion powder

1 teaspoon garlic powder

½ teaspoon dry mustard

½ teaspoon ground turmeric

AGAR GEL

1 cup cold water, filtered

1½ tablespoons agar powder

Place all the cheese ingredients in a blender, and process until the mixture becomes smooth and creamy. Leave the cheese mixture in the blender.

To make the agar gel, whisk the cold water and the agar together in a saucepan. Let it soak for 5 minutes then bring to a boil. Lower the heat and simmer, whisking often, for 5 to 8 minutes, to activate the agar.

Once the agar mixture is ready, quickly transfer it to the cheese mixture in the blender and process until it is homogenous. Pour the mixture into a round container or cake pan and cover. Refrigerate until firm and set, at least 2 to 4 hours.

Wrap the cheese in waxed paper and store in a sealed container. Will keep, refrigerated, for 1 to 2 weeks.

SWISS CHEESE

———————//———————

This firm, mild cheese with the classic, distinctive Swiss cheese taste is ideal for slicing, shredding, and melting on your favorite sandwiches.

Makes an approximately 1-pound block

PREP AND COOK TIME
under 30 minutes

WAIT TIME
2 to 4 hours

Seed-Free / Soy-Free

Tahini is a smooth, creamy paste made from sesame seeds that is used in Middle Eastern cuisine. It adds a wonderful texture and nutty flavor to many of the vegan cheese recipes.

CHEESE

½ cup raw Brazil nuts, soaked, drained, and rinsed (see page 28)

½ cup water, filtered

¼ cup nutritional yeast

3 tablespoons fresh lemon juice

2 tablespoons tahini

1 teaspoon dry mustard

½ teaspoon sea salt

½ teaspoon garlic powder

1 tablespoon onion powder

¼ teaspoon ground coriander

AGAR GEL

1 cup cold water, filtered

1½ tablespoons agar powder

Place all the cheese ingredients in a blender. Process until completely smooth. Leave the cheese mixture in the blender.

To make the agar gel, whisk the cold water and the agar together in a saucepan. Let it soak for 5 minutes then bring to a boil. Lower the heat and simmer, whisking often, for 5 to 8 minutes, to activate the agar.

Once the agar mixture is ready, quickly transfer it to the cheese mixture in the blender and process until it is homogenous. Pour into a container, cover, and let the cheese set in the refrigerator, at least 2 to 4 hours.

Wrap the cheese in waxed paper. Store in a sealed container in the refrigerator. Will keep, refrigerated, for 1 to 2 weeks.

TRICK OF THE TRADE To make the "Swiss" holes, use a drinking straw or apple corer.

JALAPEÑO JACK

———//———

Firm in texture and pleasantly spicy in flavor, this pepper Jack variety has an extra jalapeño bite. Wonderful for everyday snacking, sliced and melted on grilled panini, and cubed to top salads.

Makes an approximately 1-pound block

PREP AND COOK TIME
under 30 minutes

WAIT TIME
2 to 4 hours

Seed-Free / Soy-Free

CHEESE

½ cup raw Brazil nuts, soaked, rinsed, and drained (see page 28)

½ cup raw cashews, soaked, rinsed, and drained (see page 28)

½ cup water, filtered

3 tablespoons fresh lemon juice

3 tablespoons nutritional yeast

½ teaspoon onion powder

1 jalapeño pepper

AGAR GEL

¾ cup cold water, filtered

1 tablespoon agar powder

Place all the cheese ingredients in a blender. Process until very smooth. Leave the cheese mixture in the blender.

To make the agar gel, whisk the cold water and the agar together in a saucepan. Let it soak for 5 minutes then bring to a boil. Lower the heat and simmer, whisking often, for 5 to 8 minutes, to activate the agar.

Once the agar mixture is ready, quickly transfer it to the cheese mixture in the blender and process until it is homogenous. Pour into a container, cover, and let the cheese set in the refrigerator, at least 2 to 4 hours.

Wrap the cheese in waxed paper. Store in a sealed container in the refrigerator. Will keep, refrigerated, for 1 to 2 weeks.

APPLE-SMOKED GOUDA

———— // ————

This firm, Dutch-inspired table cheese with a distinctive smoky flavor makes for wonderful snacking. A few drops of apple-flavored liquid smoke is all that's needed to enhance its gourmet appeal.

Makes an approximately 1-pound block

PREP AND COOK TIME
under 30 minutes

WAIT TIME
2 to 4 hours

Seed-Free / Soy-Free

CHEESE

½ cup raw, blanched almonds, soaked, rinsed, and drained (see page 28)

½ cup raw cashews, soaked, rinsed, and drained (see page 28)

½ cup water, filtered

2 tablespoons fresh lemon juice

1 teaspoon pure maple syrup

1 teaspoon prepared mustard

½ teaspoon apple liquid smoke

¼ cup nutritional yeast

½ teaspoon sea salt

½ teaspoon garlic powder

1½ teaspoons onion powder

AGAR GEL

1 cup cold water, filtered

1½ tablespoons agar powder

Place all the cheese ingredients in a blender. Process until very smooth. Leave the cheese mixture in the blender.

To make the agar gel, whisk the cold water and the agar together in a saucepan. Let it soak for 5 minutes then bring to a boil. Lower the heat and simmer, whisking often, for 5 to 8 minutes, to activate the agar.

Once the agar mixture is ready, quickly transfer it to the cheese mixture in the blender and process until it is homogenous. Pour into a container, cover, and let the cheese set in the refrigerator, at least 2 to 4 hours.

Wrap the cheese in waxed paper. Store in a sealed container in the refrigerator. Will keep, refrigerated, for 1 to 2 weeks.

SMOKED CHIPOTLE

———————//———————

This smoky, firm-textured cheese with a delightful heat can be sliced, melted, and shredded. Try on top of soups or baked dishes or grated and sprinkled on baked potatoes.

*Makes an approximately
1-pound block*

PREP AND COOK TIME
under 30 minutes

WAIT TIME
2 to 4 hours

Seed-Free / Soy-Free

CHEESE

1 cup raw Brazil nuts, soaked, rinsed, and drained (see page 28)

½ cup water, filtered

3 tablespoons nutritional yeast

3 tablespoons fresh lime juice

1 tablespoon chickpea miso paste

1 teaspoon sea salt

¼ red onion, minced

1 chipotle pepper, minced

½ teaspoon liquid smoke

AGAR GEL

¾ cup cold water, filtered

1 tablespoon agar powder

Place all the cheese ingredients in a blender. Process until creamy. Leave the cheese mixture in the blender.

To make the agar gel, whisk the cold water and the agar together in a saucepan. Let it soak for 5 minutes then bring to a boil. Lower the heat and simmer, whisking often, for 5 to 8 minutes, to activate the agar.

Once the agar mixture is ready, quickly transfer it to the cheese mixture in the blender and process until it is homogenous. Pour into a container, cover, and let the cheese set in the refrigerator, at least 2 to 4 hours.

Wrap the cheese in waxed paper. Store in a sealed container in the refrigerator. Will keep, refrigerated, for 1 to 2 weeks.

TRICK OF THE TRADE For a richer-tasting cheese, use a homemade nut milk (page 33) instead of water or add 1 to 2 tablespoons of coconut or olive oil when blending.

CHAI-SPICED CHEESE

———— // ————

This creamy dessert cheese is a delight of delicately fragranced warming chai spices. Enjoy on toast at breakfast or as part of your cheese course.

Makes an approximately 1-pound block

PREP AND COOK TIME
under 30 minutes

WAIT TIME
2 to 4 hours

Seed-Free / Soy-Free

Chai tea, whether packaged or loose leaf, includes such spices as ginger, whole cloves, whole coriander, black peppercorns, green cardamom, fennel seed, cinnamon stick, and star anise.

TEA

2 teaspoons loose-leaf traditional masala chai tea leaves, or 2 chai tea bags

1¼ cups cold water, filtered

CHEESE

1 cup raw cashews, soaked, rinsed, and drained (see page 28)

2 tablespoons pure maple or raw organic agave syrup

1 tablespoon nutritional yeast

1 teaspoon chickpea miso paste

½ teaspoon sea salt

AGAR GEL

1 tablespoon agar powder

Prepare the tea: Place the loose tea leaves in a saucepan with the cold water. Bring to a boil, then lower the heat and simmer for 3 to 5 minutes. If using tea bags, bring the water to a boil, add the tea bags, and steep for 3 minutes. Let cool, then chill.

Place all the cheese ingredients, including ⅓ cup of the chilled tea, in a blender and process until smooth and creamy. Leave the cheese mixture in the blender.

To make the agar gel, whisk the remaining ⅔ cup of chilled tea and the agar powder together in a saucepan. Let it soak for 5 minutes before bringing to a boil. Lower the heat and simmer, whisking often, for 5 to 8 minutes, to activate the agar.

Once the agar mixture is ready, quickly transfer it to the cheese mixture in the blender and process until the mixture becomes homogenous. Pour into a container of your liking, keeping in mind that it will serve as the form for your cheese. Cover and let the cheese firm and set in the refrigerator, at least 2 to 4 hours.

Wrap the cheese in waxed paper. Store in a sealed container in the refrigerator, for 1 to 2 weeks.

TRICK OF THE TRADE There is no hard-and-fast rule about how long the cheese needs to culture. Temperature, humidity, and other factors can come into play. Use your taste buds to determine your preferred sharpness and tangy-ness.

MEDITERRANEAN FETA

———————//———————

Salty and briny, this traditional-style feta can be crumbled, cubed, or sliced over salads, watermelon, or a variety of your favorite savory dishes.
Stored in a brine, it keeps refrigerated for weeks. The flavor improves as it ages.

Makes an approximately 1-pound block

PREP AND COOK TIME
30 minutes

WAIT TIME
12 to 24 hours to culture, 6 to 8 hours to set, and 8 hours in brine

Seed-Free / Soy-Free

CHEESE

2 cups raw blanched almonds, soaked, rinsed, and drained (see page 28)

1 cup rejuvelac (see page 38)

1 teaspoon sea salt

AGAR GEL

⅔ cup cold water, filtered

2 tablespoons agar powder

BRINE

¼ cup sea salt

3 cups water, filtered

Place all the cheese ingredients in a blender and process until smooth. Pour the mixture into a glass container and cover with plastic wrap. Let culture at room temperature for 12 to 24 hours.

After the culturing is complete, make the agar gel: Place the cold water and the agar powder in a saucepan. Let it soak for 5 minutes before bringing to a boil. Lower the heat and simmer, whisking often, for 5 to 8 minutes, to activate the agar.

When the agar gel is ready, pour into the cultured mixture, and whisk until combined. Transfer the cheese mixture to a container lined with cheesecloth. Refrigerate for 6 to 8 hours, until firm and set.

To prepare the brine, bring 3 cups water to a boil, dissolve the salt in the boiling water, then allow to cool.

Cut the cheese into pieces and place in the salty water, then cover and leave at room temperature for 8 hours. Transfer the cheese to a container with a secured lid and pour brine over it. Store, covered, in the refrigerator for up to 6 weeks.

AGAR AND TAPIOCA TECHNIQUE

If you love gooey, stretchy, melting cheeses, you've come to the right place. The following recipes use a process of emulsification, whereby the ingredients are cooked and blended together into a homogenous mixture. Tapioca flour (aka tapioca starch) is used here as a thickening agent and is what allows the cheese to stretch as it melts.

You will need a glass or ceramic container that can hold 2 to 3 cups of liquid. This container will serve as your cheese form, so be mindful when choosing its shape.

SRIRACHA VEGETABLE CHEESE

———— // ————

This hard, smooth, flavorful cheese made of chickpeas and spiced with the delicious sriracha hot sauce is a fun vegetable table cheese to have around. It slices, grates, and shreds for endless eating possibilities.

Makes an approximately ½-pound block

PREP AND COOK TIME
30 minutes

WAIT TIME
6 to 8 hours to set

Seed-Free / Soy-Free

1 cup cooked chickpeas

¾ cup coconut milk

1 tablespoon chickpea miso paste

2 tablespoons nutritional yeast

½ teaspoon onion powder

½ teaspoon garlic powder

1 teaspoon sriracha

½ teaspoon sea salt

2 tablespoons tapioca flour

1 tablespoon agar powder

½ cup fresh cilantro, chopped

Place all the ingredients, except the cilantro, in a blender and process until smooth. Transfer the mixture to a nonstick saucepan. Heat the mixture over medium heat, continually stirring with a flexible spatula. When the mixture begins to thicken, lower the heat to low. Continue to cook, stirring, for 5 to 8 minutes, or until the mixture transforms into a stretchy, smooth, gooey mass of melted cheese.

Remove the saucepan from the heat and fold in the cilantro. Transfer the cheese to a container. Let cool for 30 minutes. Cover and refrigerate for 6 to 8 hours to firm and set.

Wrap the cheese in waxed paper. Store in a sealed container in the refrigerator. Will keep, refrigerated, for 1 to 2 weeks.

ARUGULA PESTO CHEESE

———//———

This creamy, country-style hazelnut cheese tastes as decadent as it looks. It will make the perfect centerpiece at your next wine and cheese gathering. This recipe will make more pesto than you need. For a festive presentation, brush the remaining pesto over the cheese.

Makes an approximately ½-pound block

PREP AND COOK TIME
30 minutes

WAIT TIME
12 to 24 hours to culture and 4 to 6 hours to set

Soy-Free

CHEESE

1 cup raw hazelnuts, soaked, rinsed, and drained (see page 28)

½ cup rejuvelac (see page 38)

2 tablespoons organic refined coconut oil, melted

1 teaspoon sea salt

2 tablespoons nutritional yeast

ARUGULA PESTO

1 cup arugula

2 garlic cloves

⅓ cup pine nuts

2 tablespoons extra-virgin olive oil

1 teaspoon sea salt

AGAR AND TAPIOCA MIX

½ cup hemp milk

1 tablespoon agar powder

1 tablespoon tapioca flour

Place all the cheese ingredients in a blender. Blend until smooth and creamy. Transfer the mixture to a glass container, cover with a clean kitchen towel, and let the cheese culture at room temperature for 12 to 24 hours.

Before the fermentation is complete, make the arugula pesto by processing all the pesto ingredients together in a blender until the desired consistency is reached.

After fermentation, make the agar and tapioca mix by combining the hemp milk and agar powder in a large saucepan. Bring to a simmer over low heat, whisking continually, for 5 to 8 minutes. When the agar is dissolved, pour in the cultured mixture and tapioca flour and whisk quickly. As the mixture heats and

begins to thicken, keep stirring until the mixture turns into a smooth and stretchy mass of melted cheese.

Add 1 to 2 tablespoons of the pesto and mix well. Transfer the melted cheese to a container lined with plastic wrap and cover. Refrigerate for 4 to 6 hours, until it firms and sets. Will keep, covered and refrigerated, for 1 to 2 weeks.

PROVOLONE

This firm-textured, Italian-style cheese slices beautifully and pairs exceptionally well with Italian wines and fresh fruits and vegetables.

Makes an approximately 1-pound block

PREP AND COOK TIME
30 minutes

WAIT TIME
12 to 24 hours to culture and 4 hours to set

Seed-Free / Soy-Free

VARIATIONS AND SUBSTITUTIONS For a smoky variety, prepare the recipe as directed, but add a pinch of hickory salt or several drops of liquid smoke to taste.

CHEESE

1 cup raw cashews, soaked, rinsed, and drained (see page 28)

1 cup rejuvelac (see page 38)

2 tablespoons chickpea miso paste

3 tablespoons nutritional yeast

1 teaspoon sea salt

½ teaspoon onion powder

AGAR AND TAPIOCA MIX

½ cup plus 2 tablespoons cold water, filtered

1 tablespoon agar powder

2 tablespoons tapioca flour

Place all the cheese ingredients in a blender. Process until smooth. Transfer the mixture to a container, cover with a clean kitchen towel, and let the cheese culture at room temperature for 12 to 24 hours, until the mixture has thickened. During the fermentation process the mixture will rise and develop a bubbly, airy texture.

After the culturing is complete, make the agar and tapioca mix: Place ½ cup of the cold water and the agar powder in a large saucepan and whisk to combine. Bring to a light boil, lower the heat to low, and simmer for 5 to 8 minutes, whisking continuously. Add the cultured mixture to the agar gel and whisk quickly.

In a small bowl, dissolve the tapioca flour in the remaining 2 tablespoons of cold water and add to the mixture. Cook until stretchy and shiny. Pour into a container, cover, and refrigerate until set, at least 4 hours.

Wrap the cheese in waxed paper. Store in a sealed container in the refrigerator. Will keep, refrigerated, for 2 to 3 weeks.

TRICK OF THE TRADE Ferment a minimum of 12 hours and up to 24.

FRENCH-STYLE BRIE

———— // ————

The classic French Brie is the inspiration for this creamy and buttery vegan cheese. Served at room temperature, it pairs exceptionally well with sparkling wines, fresh fruit, and crackers, or try baking it in puff pastry. Although it is not a hard cheese, the same technique that makes the provolone on page 95 melty gives this cheese its distinctive gooey texture.

Makes an approximately 1-pound round

PREP AND COOK TIME
30 minutes

WAIT TIME
24 to 48 hours to culture, 6 to 8 hours to set, and 12 to 24 hours to air dry

Seed-Free / Soy-Free

CHEESE

1 cup raw cashews, soaked, rinsed, and drained (see page 28)

1 cup water, filtered

½ cup plain unsweetened nondairy, soy-free yogurt

½ cup organic refined coconut oil, melted

1 tablespoon nutritional yeast

1 teaspoon sea salt

AGAR AND TAPIOCA MIX

4 tablespoons tapioca flour, divided

1 teaspoon agar powder

Place all the cheese ingredients in a blender and process until smooth. Transfer to a glass container and cover with a clean kitchen towel. Let the cheese culture at room temperature for 24 to 48 hours.

After culturing is complete, pour the mixture into a large saucepan. Whisk in 2 tablespoons of the tapioca flour and the agar powder and cook over medium heat, stirring constantly with a flexible spatula until the mixture is thick, glossy, and pulls away from the sides of the pan, 8 to 10 minutes.

Line a cake pan or a round glass container with cheesecloth or plastic wrap, with any excess hanging over the sides. Pour in the cheese and spread. Cool, cover, and refrigerate for 6 to 8 hours, until firm.

Once firm, lift the cheese out, remove the cheesecloth or plastic wrap, and place on a waxed paper–lined plate. Dust the cheese on all sides with the remaining 2 tablespoons of tapioca flour. Place the uncovered cheese in the refrigerator to air dry for 12 to 24 hours.

Wrap the cheese in waxed paper. Store in a sealed container in the refrigerator for 2 to 3 weeks.

Organic refined **coconut oil** provides the solid fat essential for thickening many vegan cheeses. Coconut oil becomes semisolid at room temperature and solid when chilled. It must be melted for proper measurement in recipes.

DARK CHOCOLATE BRIE

———— // ————

This decadent twist on the French classic boasts a dark chocolate flavor that is sure to wow your most discriminate guest. Enjoy with sparkling wine and berries.

Makes an approximately 1-pound round

PREP AND COOK TIME
30 minutes

WAIT TIME
12 to 24 hours to culture and 4 to 6 hours to set

Seed-Free / Soy-Free

CHEESE

2 cups raw macadamia nuts, soaked, rinsed, and drained (see page 28)

¾ cup rejuvelac (see page 38)

¼ cup organic refined coconut oil, melted

1 teaspoon sea salt

SEASONING

1 tablespoon nutritional yeast

1 tablespoon chickpea miso paste

3 tablespoons raw organic agave syrup

½ teaspoon pure vanilla extract

2 tablespoons raw cacao powder

AGAR AND TAPIOCA MIX

¾ cup almond milk

1 tablespoon agar powder

2 tablespoons tapioca flour

Place all the cheese ingredients in a blender. Blend until smooth and creamy. Transfer the mixture to a glass container, cover with a clean kitchen towel, and let the cheese culture at room temperature for 12 to 24 hours.

When the fermentation is complete, stir all the seasoning ingredients into the cultured mixture and blend well.

To make the agar and tapioca mix, mix the almond milk and agar powder in a large saucepan until well combined. Bring to a simmer over low heat, whisking continually, for 5 to 8 minutes.

When the agar is dissolved, pour in the cultured mixture and tapioca flour and whisk quickly. As the mixture heats and begins to thicken, stir with a flexible spatula. Continue to cook until the mixture trans-

forms into a smooth and stretchy mass of melted cheese. Transfer to a container lined with plastic wrap and cover. Refrigerate for 4 to 6 hours, until it firms and sets.

Wrap the cheese in waxed paper. Store in a sealed container in the refrigerator. Will keep, refrigerated, for 1 to 2 weeks.

CARRAGEENAN AND TAPIOCA TECHNIQUE

Just as with the previous technique, the following method allows for beautifully melting cheeses. Kappa carrageenan, a derivative of seaweed, is the firming agent of choice here. One of the benefits of using Kappa carrageenan is that it is heat reversible. Meaning, it can be remelted when exposed to heat even after it has been set.

When working with carrageenan, it is very important that the cheese mixture be heated sufficiently to activate the carrageenan. The entire cooking process should take five to eight minutes. If in doubt, have an instant-read thermometer handy. The cheese is ready when the temperature reaches 175°F.

It is also important to note that Kappa carrageenan is sensitive to acids. Always add your acids to the cheese mixture after emulsification has occurred.

A glass or ceramic container of your choice will be needed for shaping and firming the cheese.

An important note about carrageenan: Carrageenan is produced in three forms: Iota, Lambda, and Kappa. Lambda is widely used in commercial foods and is the type that has been linked to recent media controversy for its gastrointestinal effects. Kappa, which is molecularly different from the other two carrageenan types, is the firming agent we use here. Check the resources list (page 179) for possible suppliers.

GOLDEN CHEDDAR

———— // ————

Firm, mild, and buttery, this beautiful golden-hued Cheddar-style cheese is as superb on a cracker as it is melted on a veggie burger.

Makes an approximately 1-pound block

PREP AND COOK TIME
30 minutes

WAIT TIME
4 to 6 hours to set

Nut-Free / Seed-Free / Soy-Free

½ cup water, filtered

1 cup nondairy, soy-free yogurt

3 tablespoons tapioca flour

2 tablespoons Kappa carrageenan powder

2 tablespoons nutritional yeast

1 tablespoon chickpea miso paste

1 tablespoon tomato paste

½ teaspoon sea salt

½ teaspoon onion powder

½ teaspoon dry mustard

⅓ cup extra-virgin olive oil

2 teaspoons raw apple cider vinegar

Pour the water and yogurt into a medium saucepan, add the tapioca flour and carrageenan powder, and whisk until smooth. Add all the remaining ingredients, except the vinegar, and whisk until well blended.

Heat over medium heat, continually stirring the mixture with a flexible spatula. When it begins to thicken, lower the heat and continue to cook, stirring, for 5 to 8 minutes, or until the mixture transforms into a stretchy, smooth, gooey mass of melted cheese.

Remove the saucepan from the heat and fold in the vinegar. Transfer the melted cheese to a container and let it cool for 30 minutes before refrigerating.

Cover with plastic wrap and refrigerate for 4 to 6 hours, to allow the cheese to firm and set.

Wrap the cheese in waxed paper. Store in a sealed container in the refrigerator. Will keep, refrigerated, for 1 to 2 weeks.

TRICK OF THE TRADE Carrageenan is sensitive to acids. Too much vinegar can cause a loss in gelling capability. It can also interfere with the emulsification process. To prevent this from occurring, only add the acidic component to the cheese mixture after emulsification has occurred.

MOZZARELLA

––– // –––

This delicate vegan mozzarella, like its fresh dairy counterpart, is moist, soft, and easily melts. Make a lovely Caprese salad with fresh basil and tomatoes, or try it with a plate of delicious grilled vegetables.

Makes about 1 pound

PREP AND COOK TIME
30 minutes

WAIT TIME
4 to 6 hours to set

Seed-Free / Soy-Free

VARIATIONS AND SUBSTITUTIONS For a delicious variation, put mozzarella balls in a clear jar and top with extra-virgin olive oil infused with garlic and herbs. This makes a wonderful last-minute appetizer and can be a lovely hostess gift. Vary the herbs with the season to maximize the variety of colors and flavors.

CHEESE

1 cup plain nondairy, soy-free yogurt

1 cup raw cashews, soaked, rinsed, and drained (see page 28)

½ cup water, filtered

2 teaspoons sea salt

TAPIOCA AND CARRAGEENAN MIX

3 tablespoons tapioca flour

2 tablespoons Kappa carrageenan powder

BRINE

2 tablespoons sea salt

4 cups ice water

Place all the cheese ingredients in a blender and process until smooth and creamy. Transfer to a glass container and cover with cheesecloth. Let the cheese culture for 12 to 24 hours, until slightly tangy.

Pour the cultured cheese mixture into a saucepan, add the tapioca flour and carrageenan powder, and whisk well to combine. Cook over medium-low heat for 8 to 10 minutes, stirring with a flexible spatula, until the mixture is smooth, glossy, and stretchy.

Combine the two tablespoons salt and ice water in a bowl. Using an ice-cream scoop, drop balls of the cheese into the brine. Cover and let the cheese set in the refrigerator for at least 4 to 6 hours. Stored in the brine, the mozzarella should keep, refrigerated, for 1 to 2 weeks.

TRICK OF THE TRADE Perhaps the most exciting part about making your own cheese is being able to customize it to your own specifications. If you prefer a mozzarella in block form for instance, simply transfer the cheese mixture to a form or container of your choice right after the cooking process. No need to use the brine method.

DILL HAVARTI

The traditional Scandinavian cheese, Havarti, is known for its rich and buttery taste. Enhanced with the flavor of dill, it boasts a delicious, sophisticated flavor. This vegan Havarti is the perfect accompaniment to your cheese board. Serve with crackers or melt on your favorite grilled sandwiches.

Makes an approximately 1-pound block

PREP AND COOK TIME
30 minutes

WAIT TIME
6 to 8 hours to set

Seed-Free / Soy-Free

1⅓ cups almond milk

1 tablespoon Kappa carrageenan powder

2 tablespoons tapioca flour

1 tablespoon nutritional yeast

1 teaspoon sea salt

⅔ cup organic refined coconut oil, melted

2 teaspoons raw apple cider vinegar

2 teaspoons fresh lemon juice

2 tablespoons minced fresh dill

Place the almond milk, carrageenan powder, tapioca flour, yeast, and salt in a saucepan. Whisk vigorously until all the ingredients are well blended and the mixture is smooth. Add the coconut oil to the mixture and whisk again.

Heat over medium heat, continually stirring the mixture with a flexible spatula. When the mixture begins to thicken, lower the heat to low. Start to scrape the sides of the saucepan with the spatula while stirring vigorously. Continue to cook, stirring, for 5 to 8 minutes, until the mixture transforms into a stretchy, smooth, gooey mass of melted cheese.

Remove the saucepan from the heat and fold in the vinegar, lemon juice, and dill. Whisk to blend.

Transfer the cheese to a container. Let cool for 30 minutes. Cover and refrigerate for 6 to 8 hours, to firm and set. To store, wrap the cheese in waxed paper and refrigerate in a sealed container. Will keep for 1 to 2 weeks.

CAMEMBERT

If you love creamy, earthy French cheese with a bloomy rind, you'll love this vegan Camembert. Similar to Brie, Camembert is a nutty cheese but has deeper earthy undertones. Slice this fragrant cheese over a piece of crusty baguette or present it as part of your next cheese platter for ultimate enjoyment.

Makes an approximately 1-pound round

PREP AND COOK TIME
30 minutes

WAIT TIME
6 to 8 hours to set and 8 hours to air dry

Seed-Free / Soy-Free

VARIATIONS AND SUBSTITUTIONS For a fun and delicious treat, serve your wheel with maple-glazed pecans. Toast nuts and drizzle with maple syrup.

1⅓ cups almond milk

1½ teaspoons Kappa carrageenan powder

¼ cup plus 2 tablespoons tapioca flour

1 tablespoon nutritional yeast

1 tablespoon chickpea miso paste

1 teaspoon sea salt

½ cup organic refined coconut oil, melted

1 tablespoon raw apple cider vinegar

1 teaspoon truffle oil

Place the almond milk, carrageenan powder, ¼ cup of the tapioca flour, yeast, miso, and salt in a saucepan. Whisk vigorously until all the ingredients are well blended and the mixture is smooth. Add the coconut oil and whisk again.

Heat over medium heat, continually stirring the mixture with a flexible spatula. As the mixture begins to thicken, lower the heat to low. Scrape the sides of the saucepan with the spatula while stirring vigorously. Continue to cook, stirring, for 5 to 8 minutes, until the mixture transforms into a stretchy, smooth, gooey mass of melted cheese.

Remove the saucepan from the heat and fold in the vinegar and truffle oil. Whisk to blend.

Line a cake pan or a round glass container with plastic wrap with any extra hanging over the sides. Pour in the cheese mixture. Spread evenly and cover. Let the cheese cool for 30 minutes before refrigerating for 6 to 8 hours to firm and set.

Remove the cheese from the container and place on a waxed paper–lined plate. Dust the cheese with the remaining 2 tablespoons of tapioca flour. This will help dry the exterior and mimic the white rind you find on traditional Camembert. Place the uncovered cheese in the refrigerator to air dry for 8 hours.

Wrap the cheese in plastic wrap. Store in a sealed container in the refrigerator. Will keep, refrigerated, for 1 to 2 weeks. Allow the cheese to come to room temperature before serving.

TRICK OF THE TRADE If the heat is too high or the mixture is heated too quickly, sometimes the oil might separate from the mixture while cooking. If this occurs, remove the saucepan from the heat and stir vigorously until smooth. If the mixture will not reemulsify, add a dash of almond milk and whisk until recombined.

Citrus and/or Vinegar Technique

Pesto Ricotta • Herbed Farmer Cheese • Boursin-Style Garlic and Herb
Ricotta • Festive Two-Nut Cheese Ball • Herbed Feta • Baked Feta
Gorgonzola • Triple Peppercorn Cheese • Pumpkin Cheesecake

Probiotic Technique

Olive and Roasted Pepper Cheese Terrine • Mustard-Horseradish Encrusted Cheese
Olive and Sun-Dried Tomato • Herbes de Provence Cheese
Chèvre Noir • Maple-Fig Double Cream • Sweet Italian Mascarpone

Rejuvelac Technique

Quick-and-Easy Cream Cheese • Classic Cream Cheese
Habanero-Smoked Farmhouse Cheese • Herbed Fondue • Thai Spice Double Cream
Aged Gruyère • Creamy Danish Blue • Drunken Goat • Cheese Truffles

SOFT AND FRESH CHEESES

―――――――――――――――――――――――――――――――

FOR CHEESE LOVERS WHO PREFER SOFT, SPREADABLE CHEESES, THIS category is sure to please. The cheeses in this section are made using vinegar and citrus juices to create fresh and unripened varieties, such as cream cheese, ricotta, and farmer cheese. These cheeses make great spreads, and can also be firmed up and dehydrated to form a rind. Some recipes use rejuvelac and probiotics as culturing agents to create ripened varieties, such as goat and blue cheeses.

When preparing to make fully sharp, pungent, or ripe varieties, rejuvelac is an obvious choice. Make sure to give yourself three to six days to prepare the fermented liquid, however. You'll have to plan your recipes accordingly or always keep enough on hand. Preparing rejuvelac at home is simple to do. Just follow my instructions on page 38. You can also find a ready-made rejuvelac in your health food store. Check the resources at the end of this book for possible suppliers (page 179).

As an alternative, you can swap probiotic powder for rejuvelac. A teaspoon of probiotics is equivalent to six to eight capsules of the friendly bacteria found in your health food store's supplements department. Simply open the capsules and empty the powder into a small bowl. Probiotics don't require any advance preparation, making this one of the simplest methods, albeit a more expensive one, to prepare vegan cultured cheeses.

CITRUS AND/OR VINEGAR TECHNIQUE

PESTO RICOTTA

This elegant and fragrant pine nut ricotta can be used as a lovely dip or spread, or can be thinned down with almond milk and tossed with zucchini noodles for a tasty dinner.

Makes a 10- to 12-ounce soft round

PREP AND COOK TIME
15 minutes

WAIT TIME
4 to 6 hours

Soy-Free

2 cups raw pine nuts, soaked, rinsed, and drained (see page 28)

3 tablespoons fresh lemon juice

2 tablespoons nutritional yeast

2 garlic cloves, peeled

½ cup fresh basil, minced

1 teaspoon sea salt

¼ to ½ cup almond milk

Place all the ingredients in a blender, starting with ¼ cup of the almond milk. Pulse, adding more liquid as necessary, until fluffy. Transfer to a glass container, cover, and refrigerate for 4 to 6 hours to chill and set.

Store the ricotta in an airtight container in the refrigerator. Will keep, refrigerated, for 5 to 7 days.

HERBED FARMER CHEESE

————//————

Soft, spreadable, and delicious, this savory nut cheese infused with lime and dill spreads easily to enjoy on a crisp cracker or a piece of crusty bread.

Makes an approximately 8-ounce soft round

PREP AND COOK TIME
15 minutes

WAIT TIME
8 to 12 hours

Seed-Free / Soy-Free

1 cup raw cashews, soaked, rinsed, and drained (see page 28)

2 tablespoons fresh lime juice

2 tablespoons organic refined coconut oil, melted

3 tablespoons almond milk

½ teaspoon sea salt

¼ teaspoon freshly ground white pepper

¼ cup fresh dill, minced

Place all the ingredients, except the dill, in a blender. Blend until creamy and smooth. Add the dill and stir to combine.

Scoop the cheese mixture into a form lined with cheesecloth or plastic wrap. Pack firmly. Cover with plastic wrap and refrigerate for at least 8 to 12 hours, or until the cheese is set and firm.

Wrap the cheese in plastic wrap. Store in a sealed container in the refrigerator. Will keep, refrigerated, for 1 to 2 weeks. The flavor will continue to develop as the cheese ages.

TRICK OF THE TRADE To melt the coconut oil, place the jar of coconut oil in about an inch of hot water for a few minutes. Repeated melting and hardening will not harm the oil.

BOURSIN-STYLE GARLIC AND HERB

A creamy blend of delicate roasted garlic and savory herbs makes this Boursin-style cheese an irresistibly spreadable delight perfect for everyday entertaining.

Makes an approximately 8-ounce soft round

PREP AND COOK TIME
40 minutes

WAIT TIME
8 to 12 hours

Seed-Free / Soy-Free

3 garlic cloves, peeled and roasted

¼ cup chopped fresh herbs; e.g., thyme, rosemary, chives

1 cup raw cashews, soaked, rinsed, and drained (see page 28)

½ teaspoon sea salt

3 tablespoons fresh lemon juice

3 tablespoons coconut milk

Preheat the oven to 350°F. Wrap the garlic in aluminum foil and roast for 30 minutes, or until fragrant and tender.

Place all the ingredients in a blender and process until smooth.

Line a form with cheesecloth. Transfer the cheese mixture to the lined form and pack, using the back of a spoon. Cover and refrigerate overnight.

Remove the cheese from the lined form. Wrap the cheese in plastic wrap. Store in the refrigerator. Will keep, refrigerated, for 1 to 2 weeks.

RICOTTA

Ricotta cheese, the delicious key ingredient in Italian dishes from lasagne to cannoli, is simple to re-create in your own vegan kitchen. Mild and creamy with a hint of sweetness.

Makes a 10- to 12-ounce soft round

PREP AND COOK TIME
15 minutes

WAIT TIME
4 to 6 hours

Seed-Free / Soy-Free

2 cups raw macadamia nuts, soaked, rinsed, and drained (see page 28)

1 teaspoon sea salt

2 tablespoons fresh lemon juice

½ cup water, filtered

Place all the ingredients in a blender. Pulse until fluffy, adding more water if necessary. Transfer to a glass container, cover, and refrigerate for 4 to 6 hours to chill and set.

Store the ricotta in an airtight container in the refrigerator. Will keep, refrigerated, for 5 to 7 days.

TRICK OF THE TRADE For a richer taste and consistency, replace the water with a nondairy, soy-free milk of your choosing.

FESTIVE
TWO-NUT
CHEESE BALL

———//———

This sharp and tangy creamy
cheese is delightful as is or
can be rolled in a variety
of chopped nuts, dried fruit, or
mixed herbs to dress it up
for your most glamorous affairs.

*Makes an approximately
1-pound soft round*

PREP AND COOK TIME
15 minutes

WAIT TIME
6 to 8 hours

Soy-Free

TRICK OF THE TRADE If your
blender is struggling to blend the mixture, add more coconut or almond
milk or water, 1 tablespoon at a time,
to help it keep turning over, adding no
more than 3 tablespoons.

CHEESE

1 cup raw, blanched almonds, soaked, rinsed, and
   drained (see page 28)

1 cup raw pine nuts, soaked, rinsed, and drained (see
   page 28)

¼ cup nutritional yeast

1 tablespoon chickpea miso paste

2 tablespoons fresh lime juice

1 teaspoon sea salt

1 teaspoon onion powder

½ teaspoon garlic powder

¼ teaspoon ground turmeric

¼ cup organic refined coconut oil, melted

2 chipotle peppers

½ cup coconut or almond milk

COATING

Chopped nuts or dried fruit, or mixed herbs

Place all the cheese ingredients in a blender and process until the mixture is completely smooth, scraping
down the sides occasionally.

Place the cheese mixture in a container. Cover and
refrigerate for 6 to 8 hours to let chill and set.

Lay out a piece of plastic wrap and place half of the
cheese in the center. Form the cheese into an even, sym-
metrical shape of your liking by rolling it gently inside
the plastic wrap. Repeat with the remaining cheese.

Roll the cheese in a variety of chopped nuts or
dried fruit, or mixed herbs.

Wrap the cheese in plastic wrap. Will keep, refrigerated, for 1 to 2 weeks. Allow the cheese to soften at
room temperature before serving.

HERBED FETA

This tofu-based cheese is reminiscent of feta in both taste and texture. It is tangy and salty and is wonderful served with falafel and other Mediterranean favorites. Crumbled or cubed feta drizzled with olive oil is especially lovely on salads and on hummus.

Makes about ½ pound

PREP AND COOK TIME
15 minutes

WAIT TIME
6 to 8 hours

Nut-Free / Seed-Free

7 ounces extra-firm tofu

¼ cup organic refined coconut oil, melted

4 teaspoons fresh lemon juice

1 tablespoon raw apple cider vinegar

1 tablespoon sea salt

½ teaspoon onion powder

½ teaspoon dried oregano

½ teaspoon dried marjoram

1 teaspoon dried basil

Drain and press the tofu to release all its liquid. Crumble the tofu into a blender. Add the melted coconut oil, lemon juice, vinegar, salt, and onion powder, and process until smooth. Add the dried herbs and pulse to combine.

Transfer the cheese mixture to a container lined with plastic wrap or cheesecloth and pack it with a spatula, smoothing the surface. Cover and refrigerate for 6 to 8 hours to set and firm.

Wrap the cheese in plastic wrap. Store in a sealed container in the refrigerator. Will keep, refrigerated, for 1 to 2 weeks.

Tofu, or bean curd, is made from coagulated soy milk that has been pressed into a soft white block. Because firm tofu has less water content than softer tofu, it is higher in protein, fat, and calcium and holds up better in these cheese recipes.

BAKED FETA

Creamy on the inside with a delightful baked nutty crust on the outside, this flavorful vegan feta is remarkably similar to the real thing. Pair it with fruit at your next dinner party or enjoy it with your favorite glass of wine.

Makes 10 to 12 ounces

PREP AND COOK TIME
55 minutes

WAIT TIME
12 hours to set

Seed-Free / Soy-Free

2 cups raw, blanched almonds, soaked, rinsed, and drained (see page 28)

¼ cup fresh lemon juice

¾ cup water, filtered

¼ cup extra-virgin olive oil, plus more for pan

2 garlic cloves, peeled and minced

1½ teaspoons sea salt

Place all the ingredients in a blender and process until creamy and smooth.

Line a strainer with cheesecloth and place over a bowl. Spoon the mixture into the lined strainer. Cover and place in the refrigerator for 12 hours to firm and set.

Once the cheese has set, preheat the oven to 350°F.

Unwrap the cheese from the cheesecloth. Transfer the cheese to an oiled pan and bake for about 40 minutes, or until golden and firm to the touch. Let cool in the pan.

Wrap the cheese in waxed paper. Store in a sealed container in the refrigerator. Will keep, refrigerated, for 1 to 2 weeks.

Extra-virgin olive oil is the product of the first pressing of tree-ripened olives. It is extracted using a low temperature and chemical-free process that involves only mechanical pressure. Extra-virgin olive oil is rich in healthful monounsaturated fats.

GORGONZOLA

The salty flavor and strong bite of the classic Italian blue cheese is captured beautifully in this superb tofu-based cheese. You'll love the pungent, tangy flavor of this vegan variety. Impress your guests by serving this beauty as part of a cheese plate with fruit and crackers or crumbled on top of a pear and arugula salad.

Makes about ½ pound

PREP AND COOK TIME
15 minutes

WAIT TIME
6 to 8 hours

Nut-Free / Seed-Free

7 ounces extra-firm tofu

¼ cup organic refined coconut oil, melted

1 tablespoon fresh lemon juice

1 tablespoon white wine vinegar

2 tablespoons white miso paste

1 teaspoon sea salt

½ teaspoon onion powder

½ teaspoon garlic powder

⅛ teaspoon spirulina

Drain and press the tofu to release its liquid. Place all the ingredients, except the spirulina, in a blender, and process until smooth.

Transfer the mixture to a bowl, dot the cheese with the spirulina, and fold it over a few times to create the blue-green veins.

Place the cheese mixture in a container lined with plastic wrap and pack it with a spatula, smoothing the surface. Cover and refrigerate for 6 to 8 hours to firm and set.

Wrap the cheese in plastic wrap. Store in a sealed container in the refrigerator. Will keep, refrigerated, for 1 to 2 weeks. The flavor will continue to develop as it ages.

Spirulina, a blue-green algae found in pristine freshwater lakes, ponds, and rivers, is also what gives the blue-green veins in these vegan blue cheese recipes. Spirulina is known for its ability to strengthen the immune system.

TRIPLE PEPPERCORN CHEESE

---//---

Wake up your taste buds
with this fragrant, spicy peppercorn
cheese. Creamy and delightful,
it is delicious on its own, crumbled
on a salad, or to add a gentle kick
to your morning bagel.

Makes about 8 ounces

PREP AND COOK TIME
15 minutes

WAIT TIME
*8 hours to set and 6 to 8
hours to develop flavor*

Seed-Free / Soy-Free

1 cup raw, blanched almonds, soaked, rinsed, and
    drained (see page 28)

½ cup water, filtered

2 tablespoons extra-virgin olive oil

3 tablespoons fresh lemon juice

1 garlic clove, peeled

½ teaspoon sea salt

Peppercorn blend for topping

Place all the ingredients, except the peppercorns, in a
blender and process until smooth and creamy.

Place a strainer lined with cheesecloth over a
bowl and transfer the nut mixture to the lined strainer.
Squeeze out any excess liquid and place the cheese in
the refrigerator for 8 hours to firm and set.

Once the cheese has set, lay out a sheet of plastic
wrap on the counter and sprinkle it with the peppercorn
blend. Scoop the cheese from the cheesecloth onto the
center of the peppercorn-covered plastic wrap, twist
the ends tightly, and form the cheese into a ball or a log.
Refrigerate for 6 to 8 hours to develop flavor.

Store in a sealed container in the refrigerator. Will
keep, refrigerated, for 1 to 2 weeks.

PUMPKIN CHEESECAKE

———— // ————

No cheese book is complete without a recipe for homemade cheesecake. Especially when it's this easy to prepare. With hints of lemon and maple syrup, this tangy, sweet, and creamy vegan pumpkin cheesecake is perfect for any holiday feast. A simple nut crust creates great flavor and texture.

Makes an approximately 8-inch cake

PREP AND COOK TIME
30 minutes

WAIT TIME
3 to 4 hours to chill and overnight to set

Seed-Free / Soy-Free

CRUST

1 cup raw hazelnuts, soaked, rinsed, and drained (see page 28)

4 to 6 tablespoons blackstrap molasses

½ cup raw cacao powder

1 teaspoon pure vanilla extract

PUMPKIN CHEESECAKE

2 cups raw cashews, soaked, rinsed, and drained (see page 28)

1½ cups cooked pumpkin

⅔ cup organic refined coconut oil, melted

½ cup pure maple syrup

¼ cup fresh lemon juice

1 teaspoon pure vanilla extract

1 teaspoon sea salt

½ teaspoon ground cinnamon

½ teaspoon grated nutmeg

To make the crust, place the nuts, molasses, cacao powder, and vanilla in a blender and process until the mixture reaches the desired texture. Scoop out the mixture and press evenly into a cake pan. Let chill for 3 to 4 hours.

When the crust has chilled, make the pumpkin cheesecake filling: Place all the cheesecake ingredients in a blender. Process until the mixture is smooth and creamy. If the mixture is too thick to blend, add nondairy, soy-free milk, 1 tablespoon at a time, until the mixture thins slightly. Pour the mixture into the chilled crust, smoothing out the top. Cover and place in the refrigerator overnight to set.

The pumpkin cheesecake will keep, refrigerated, for up to 5 days.

PROBIOTIC TECHNIQUE

Probiotics are friendly bacteria often taken in capsule form as a health supplement to boost your immune system and increase nutrient absorption. The powder is used in the following recipes as the starter for culturing the nuts and seeds. Simply open a probiotic capsule and empty the powder into a small bowl. A teaspoon is usually equivalent to six to eight capsules.

You should have a mason jar handy for the majority of these recipes. When filled with water, it will make the perfect weight to press the excess moisture out of the cheese while it cultures.

OLIVE AND ROASTED PEPPER CHEESE TERRINE

———— // ————

This beautiful cheese terrine, layered with olive and roasted pepper tapenades, makes a delicious and elegant holiday appetizer. Serve with an assortment of crisps, crackers, and breads.

Makes about 1 pound

PREP AND COOK TIME
30 minutes

WAIT TIME
24 to 48 hours to culture, 6 to 8 hours to set, and 4 to 6 hours to develop flavor

Seed-Free / Soy-Free

CHEESE

1 cup raw cashews, soaked, rinsed, and drained (see page 28)

1 cup raw Brazil nuts, soaked, rinsed, and drained (see page 28)

3 tablespoons raw apple cider vinegar

3 tablespoons fresh lemon juice

½ cup water, filtered

1 teaspoon probiotic powder

SEASONING

3 tablespoons nutritional yeast

1 teaspoon sea salt

1 tablespoon chickpea miso paste

Place all the cheese ingredients in a blender. Process, starting with ½ cup of the water and slowly adding as needed, until a smooth and creamy consistency is achieved.

Place a strainer lined with cheesecloth over a bowl. Transfer the cheese mixture to the lined strainer, and twist the ends of the cheesecloth together and secure with a rubber band or twine. Place a plate on top of the wrapped cheese ball and add a weight on top, such as a mason jar filled with water, heavy enough to gently press the extra liquid out of the cheese. Cover the mixture with a clean kitchen towel and allow to culture for 24 to 48 hours at room temperature.

After fermentation is complete, unwrap the cheese and place it in a glass bowl. Add the seasoning ingredients and mix to combine. Taste, and adjust to your liking. Cover and refrigerate for 6 to 8 hours, until the cheese is very firm.

OLIVE TAPENADE

1 cup pitted Niçoise or kalamata olives

2 tablespoons chopped capers

1 tablespoon minced garlic

A few grinds of black pepper

1 tablespoon grated orange zest

4 to 6 tablespoons extra-virgin olive oil

ROASTED PEPPER TAPENADE

1 cup roasted sweet red pepper

2 teaspoons extra-virgin olive oil

1 teaspoon balsamic vinegar

½ teaspoon onion powder

½ teaspoon sea salt

¼ teaspoon freshly ground pepper

For each tapenade, place all its ingredients in a blender and process until pureed. The tapenades will keep, covered and refrigerated, for 1 to 2 weeks.

To form the terrine, separate the cheese mixture in three equal amounts. Line a small loaf pan with plastic wrap extending over all the sides. Place one-third of the cheese into the lined pan and pack firmly with the back of a spoon.

Spread the olive tapenade on top, cover with a second layer of cheese, add the roasted red pepper tapenade, and layer with the remaining cheese.

Cover with the plastic wrap and refrigerate for 4 to 6 hours, until firm.

Unwrap carefully and place on a serving plate. Slice and serve.

Will keep, covered and refrigerated, for 3 to 5 days.

MUSTARD-HORSERADISH ENCRUSTED CHEESE

———//———

This silken, semisoft seed cheese is encrusted with a flavorful layer of blended grainy mustard and horseradish, perfectly suited for entertaining and snacking alike.

Makes about 1 pound

PREP AND COOK TIME
15 minutes

WAIT TIME
*24 to 48 hours to culture,
4 to 6 hours to set, and
4 hours to develop flavor*

Nut-Free / Soy-Free

CHEESE

2 cups raw sunflower seeds, soaked, rinsed, and drained (see page 28)

1 teaspoon sea salt

¾ cup water, filtered

1 teaspoon probiotic powder

SEASONING

2 tablespoons fresh lemon juice

2 tablespoons nutritional yeast

½ teaspoon onion powder

½ teaspoon garlic powder

½ teaspoon ground turmeric

½ teaspoon ground cumin

COATING

1 tablespoon whole-grain Dijon mustard

1 tablespoon grated horseradish

Place all the cheese ingredients in a blender. Process, starting with ½ cup of the water and slowly adding more as needed, until a smooth and creamy consistency is achieved.

Place a strainer lined with cheesecloth over a bowl. Transfer the cheese mixture into the lined strainer, and twist the ends of the cheesecloth together and secure with a rubber band or twine. Place a plate on top of the wrapped cheese ball and add a weight on top, such as a mason jar filled with water, heavy enough to gently press the extra liquid out of the cheese. Cover the mixture with a clean kitchen towel and allow to culture for 24 to 48 hours at room temperature.

After fermentation is complete, unwrap the cheese and place it in a glass bowl. Add the seasoning ingredients. Mix to combine. Taste, and adjust to your liking.

Form the cheese in any shape or use a mold of your choice. Refrigerate for 4 to 6 hours to let chill and set.

Once it sets, coat the cheese with the mustard and horseradish and let rest in the refrigerator for an additional 4 hours to develop flavor. Store in a sealed container in the refrigerator. Will keep, refrigerated, for 1 to 2 weeks.

OLIVE AND SUN-DRIED TOMATO

————//————

A creamy, robust cheese filled with deep Mediterranean flavors. Serve with crackers, or toss with pasta for an instant creamy sauce.

Makes about 1 pound

PREP AND COOK TIME
15 minutes

WAIT TIME
24 to 48 hours to culture and 6 to 8 hours to set and develop flavor

Seed-Free / Soy-Free

CHEESE

1 cup raw, blanched almonds, soaked, rinsed, and drained (see page 28)

1 cup raw cashews, soaked, rinsed, and drained (see page 28)

¾ cup water, filtered

1 teaspoon probiotic powder

SEASONING

½ teaspoon sea salt

2 tablespoons nutritional yeast

1 tablespoon fresh-squeezed lemon juice

¼ cup olives, chopped

½ cup sun-dried tomatoes, soaked and drained, chopped

To make the cheese, place the nuts, water, and probiotic powder in a blender and process until smooth. Place a strainer lined with cheesecloth over a bowl. Transfer the cheese mixture to the lined strainer, and twist the ends of the cheesecloth together and secure with a rubber band or twine. Place a plate on top of the wrapped cheese ball and add a weight on top, such as a mason jar filled with water, heavy enough to gently press the extra liquid out of the cheese. Cover the mixture with a clean kitchen towel and allow to culture for 24 to 48 hours at room temperature.

After fermentation is complete, transfer the cheese to a bowl and stir in the seasoning ingredients. Mix well with a flexible spatula. Line a container with plastic wrap or cheesecloth, keeping in mind that it will serve as a form to shape the cheese. Spoon the cheese into the container and pack it tightly. Cover and refrigerate for 6 to 8 hours to let firm and set.

Wrap the cheese in plastic wrap. Store in a sealed container in the refrigerator. Will keep, refrigerated, for 1 to 2 weeks.

HERBES DE PROVENCE CHEESE

This creamy, elegant, cheese with aromatic herbs, including thyme, rosemary, tarragon, and the sweet, delicate and soothing nuances of lavender can be stirred into a pan of steamed green beans, enjoyed over salads, or served with crispy flatbread.

Makes about 1 pound

PREP AND COOK TIME
15 minutes

WAIT TIME
24 to 48 hours to culture and 8 to 12 hours to set and develop flavor

Seed-Free / Soy-Free

CHEESE

2 cups raw cashews, soaked, rinsed, and drained (see page 28)

⅔ cup cashew milk

1 teaspoon sea salt

1 teaspoon probiotic powder

SEASONING

1 tablespoon chickpea miso paste

3 tablespoons nutritional yeast

2 teaspoons herbes de Provence, plus more for topping

2 tablespoons extra-virgin olive oil

Place all the cheese ingredients in a blender and process until the mixture is completely smooth.

Place a strainer lined with cheesecloth over a bowl. Transfer the cheese mixture to the lined strainer, and twist the ends of the cheesecloth together and secure with a rubber band or twine. Place a plate on top of the wrapped cheese ball and add a weight on top, such as a mason jar filled with water, heavy enough to gently press the extra liquid out of the cheese. Cover the mixture with a clean kitchen towel and allow to culture for 24 to 48 hours at room temperature.

After fermentation is complete, unwrap the cheese and place it in a glass bowl. Add the seasoning ingredients and mix to combine. Taste, and adjust to your liking.

Press into a form lined with plastic wrap. Sprinkle with additional herbs, cover, and refrigerate for 8 to 12 hours to firm and set.

Wrap the cheese in plastic wrap. Store in a sealed container in the refrigerator. Will keep, refrigerated, for 1 to 2 weeks.

CHÈVRE NOIR

This soft, creamy cheese inspired by the French chèvre is sprinkled with exotic, savory dulse flakes for a unique taste experience. It makes an exceptionally mouthwatering match for any cheese platter.

Makes about 1 pound

PREP AND COOK TIME
15 minutes

WAIT TIME
24 to 48 hours to culture and 6 to 8 hours to set and develop flavor

Seed-Free / Soy-Free

Dulse flakes are salty sea vegetables eaten fresh and dried in such foods as soups, chowders, and fish dishes. Dulse is packed with valuable minerals, including iron and potassium.

CHEESE

2 cups raw macadamia nuts, soaked, rinsed, and drained (see page 28)

1 teaspoon probiotic powder

¾ cup water, filtered

SEASONING

2 tablespoons nutritional yeast

1 teaspoon sea salt

1 tablespoon raw apple cider vinegar

Dulse flakes for topping

Place all the cheese ingredients in a blender and process until smooth.

Place a strainer lined with cheesecloth over a bowl. Transfer the cheese mixture to the lined strainer, and twist the ends of the cheesecloth together and secure with a rubber band or twine. Place a plate on top of the wrapped cheese ball and add a weight on top, such as a mason jar filled with water, heavy enough to gently press the extra liquid out of the cheese. Cover the mixture with a clean kitchen towel and allow to culture for 24 to 48 hours at room temperature.

Transfer the mixture to a bowl and stir in the seasoning ingredients. Mix well with a flexible spatula. Line a container with plastic wrap or cheesecloth, keeping in mind that it will serve as a form to shape the cheese. Spoon the cheese into the container and pack it tightly. Cover and refrigerate for 6 to 8 hours to let firm and set.

Once the cheese has set, sprinkle with dulse flakes.

Wrap the cheese in plastic wrap. Store in a sealed container in the refrigerator. Will keep, refrigerated, for 1 to 2 weeks.

TRICK OF THE TRADE For a tangier cheese, allow to culture for up to 72 hours.

MAPLE-FIG DOUBLE CREAM

———//———

Buttery and bursting with sweet flavor, this exquisite dessert cheese is remarkable on a cheese plate served with champagne and fruit, or at brunch with brioche and coffee.

Makes about 1 pound

PREP AND COOK TIME
15 minutes

WAIT TIME
24 to 48 hours to culture and 6 to 8 hours to set and develop flavor

Seed-Free / Soy-Free

VARIATIONS Mix in chopped dried fruits, such as apricots, sour cherries, or goji berries, and aromatics, such as freshly grated nutmeg or ground cinnamon.

CHEESE

2 cups raw cashews, soaked, rinsed, and drained (see page 28)

¾ cup water, filtered

1 teaspoon probiotic powder

SEASONING

2 tablespoons nutritional yeast

1 teaspoon sea salt

2 tablespoons fresh lemon juice

½ cup chopped dried figs, soaked

3 tablespoons pure maple syrup

To make the cheese, place the nuts, water, and probiotics in a blender. Process until creamy and smooth.

Place a strainer lined with cheesecloth over a bowl. Transfer the cheese mixture to the lined strainer, and twist the ends of the cheesecloth together and secure with a rubber band or twine. Place a plate on top of the wrapped cheese ball and add a weight on top, such as a mason jar filled with water, heavy enough to gently press the extra liquid out of the cheese. Cover the mixture with a clean kitchen towel and allow to culture for 24 to 48 hours at room temperature.

After fermentation is complete, transfer the cheese to a bowl and stir in the seasoning ingredients. Mix well with a flexible spatula.

Line a container with plastic wrap or cheesecloth, it will serve as a form to shape the cheese. Spoon the cheese into the container and pack it tightly. Cover and refrigerate for 6 to 8 hours to let firm and set.

Wrap the cheese in plastic wrap. Store in a sealed container in the refrigerator. Will keep, refrigerated, for 1 to 2 weeks.

SWEET ITALIAN MASCARPONE

———— // ————

This sweet, delicate dessert cheese, best known as the main ingredient in the classic Italian tiramisu, is a delight straight out of the jar. It can also be enjoyed with fruit, in crepes, and as a creamy dessert topping.

Makes about 2 cups

PREP AND COOK TIME
15 minutes

WAIT TIME
24 to 48 hours to culture and 4 to 6 hours to set

Seed-Free / Soy-Free

½ cup water, filtered

2 cups raw cashews, rinsed, soaked, and drained (see page 28)

¼ cup fresh lemon juice

3 tablespoons pure maple syrup

1 teaspoon nutritional yeast

1 teaspoon chickpea miso paste

½ teaspoon sea salt

1 teaspoon probiotic powder

Place all the ingredients in a blender and process until smooth and creamy. Transfer the mixture to a glass container, cover, and let sit at room temperature for 24 to 48 hours to culture.

After fermentation is complete, refrigerate for 4 to 6 hours to firm and set.

Transfer the cheese into a jar or other airtight container. Will keep, refrigerated, for up to 1 week.

SERVING SUGGESTION For a decadent treat, make a quick and easy version of the Italian classic tiramisu. Simply layer mascarpone, espresso, and coconut whipped cream in individual cups. Dust with raw cacao powder and serve with ladyfinger-style sweet sponge biscuits.

REJUVELAC TECHNIQUE

Rejuvelac is a nonalcoholic fermented liquid made from grain. It is the culturing agent of choice in the following recipes. If you plan on making your own, give yourself three to six days for the rejuvelac to sprout and ferment. I offer an easy do-it-yourself recipe on page 38.

QUICK-AND-EASY CREAM CHEESE

This is the fastest way to your favorite creamy spread. If you need cream cheese on your bagel right now, this is the recipe for you.

Makes about 1 pound

PREP AND COOK TIME
15 minutes

WAIT TIME
Ready immediately

Seed-Free / Soy-Free

2 cups raw cashews, soaked, rinsed, and drained (see page 28)

2 tablespoons raw apple cider vinegar

2 tablespoons fresh lemon juice

2 tablespoons water, filtered, plus more as needed

1 teaspoon sea salt

2 tablespoons nutritional yeast

Place all the ingredients in a blender and process until the mixture is smooth and creamy. It will be thick. Scrape down the sides of the blender as necessary. Add additional water 1 tablespoon at a time, as needed.

Store the cheese in a sealed container in the refrigerator. Will keep, refrigerated, for 1 to 2 weeks.

Raw apple cider vinegar is produced from organic and unpasteurized apple cider. The "mother" of the vinegar is made up of yeasts and fermentation by-products produced when the cider ferments to vinegar. It will settle at the bottom of the bottle between uses. Be sure to shake the bottle well before pouring. You want the healthy ingredients it contains.

CLASSIC CREAM CHEESE

———//———

Your favorite morning spread is here. I offer two different recipes for vegan cream cheese: a quick-and-easy version (page 151) for when you just can't wait, and this classic one for when you have time to plan ahead. They are both quite simple, although the classic version requires some extra wait time. Try them both to see which one you prefer!

Makes about 1 pound

PREP AND COOK TIME
15 minutes

WAIT TIME
24 hours to culture and 12 hours to set and develop flavor

Seed-Free / Soy-Free

2 cups raw cashews, soaked, rinsed, and drained (see page 28)

½ cup rejuvelac (see page 38)

¼ cup organic refined coconut oil, melted

1 teaspoon sea salt

Place all the ingredients in a blender and process until smooth and creamy. Transfer the mixture to a glass container, cover, and let culture at room temperature for 24 hours.

After culturing is complete, stir the cheese, cover, and refrigerate for 12 hours to chill, firm, and develop flavor.

Store the cheese in a sealed container in the refrigerator. Will keep, refrigerated, for 1 to 2 weeks.

TRICK OF THE TRADE If you choose to infuse your cream cheese with savory flavors, you should add your herbs and spices after culturing and before chilling.

If you choose to add fruit preserves, add them after the cheese is firmed and chilled.

HABANERO-SMOKED FARMHOUSE CHEESE

———— // ————

This creamy smoked cheese is a pure delight. Spicy and tangy, it's a real crowd-pleaser. Serve on crackers or use as a delicious sandwich spread.

Makes about 1 pound

PREP AND COOK TIME
15 minutes

WAIT TIME
24 to 48 hours to culture and 8 hours to set and develop flavor

Seed-Free / Soy-Free

CHEESE

1 cup raw cashews, soaked, rinsed, and drained (see page 28)

1 cup raw Brazil nuts, soaked, rinsed, and drained (see page 28)

1 teaspoon sea salt

⅔ cup rejuvelac (see page 38)

SEASONING

2 tablespoons nutritional yeast

1 tablespoon chickpea miso paste

½ teaspoon minced garlic

1 habanero pepper, seeded and chopped

½ teaspoon liquid smoke

Place all the cheese ingredients in a blender. Process until smooth and creamy.

Transfer the cheese mixture to a glass bowl and cover with a clean kitchen towel. Let culture at room temperature for 24 to 48 hours.

After fermentation is complete, transfer the cultured mixture to a bowl, add the seasoning ingredients, and mix well to incorporate. Scoop the cheese mixture into a form lined with cheesecloth or plastic wrap and pack firmly. Cover and refrigerate at least 8 hours, or until the cheese is set and firm.

Wrap the cheese in plastic wrap. Store in a sealed container in the refrigerator. Will keep, refrigerated, for 1 to 2 weeks. The cheese will continue to firm up and slightly sharpen with age.

HERBED FONDUE

This sophisticated, luscious fondue mingles seamlessly with the decadent full-bodied flavors of rich herbs and crisp wine. Serve with ciabatta, whole-grain flatbreads, and raw vegetables.

Makes about 4 cups

PREP AND COOK TIME
30 minutes

WAIT TIME
12 to 24 hours to culture

Seed-Free / Soy-Free

CHEESE

2 cups raw macadamia nuts, soaked, rinsed, and drained (see page 28)

¼ cup organic refined coconut oil, melted

¼ cup rejuvelac (see page 38)

1 teaspoon sea salt

FONDUE

¼ cup fresh parsley

¼ cup fresh cilantro

¼ cup fresh dill

2 garlic cloves

1 cup dry white wine

3 tablespoons tapioca flour

1 cup nondairy, soy-free milk

Salt and freshly ground black pepper

Place all the cheese ingredients in a blender. Process until smooth and creamy. Transfer the mixture to a glass container and cover. Let culture for 12 to 24 hours at room temperature.

After the cheese has cultured, make the fondue:

Finely chop the parsley, cilantro, dill, and garlic and set aside.

Bring the wine to a boil in a medium saucepan. Simmer for 2 minutes, whisk in the cheese mixture, and cook for 3 to 5 minutes over low heat.

To make the fondue, in a small bowl, dissolve the tapioca in the milk. Add the tapioca mixture to the cheese mixture and cook, whisking constantly, for 3 to 5 minutes more, until thickened and smooth. Stir in the herbs and season with salt and pepper to taste, if desired.

THAI SPICE DOUBLE CREAM

This creamy round packs a savory and tangy ginger, cilantro, and lime bite. It's a sure crowd-pleaser. Enjoy on crisps and flatbreads, smothered on baked potatoes, and melted on your favorite noodles.

Makes about 1 pound

PREP AND COOK TIME
30 minutes

WAIT TIME
24 to 48 hours to culture and 6 to 8 hours to set and develop flavor

Seed-Free / Soy-Free

CHEESE

2 cups raw macadamia nuts, soaked, rinsed, and drained (see page 28)

¾ cup rejuvelac (see page 38)

1 teaspoon sea salt

SEASONING

1 teaspoon grated fresh ginger

2 tablespoons nutritional yeast

2 tablespoons fresh lime juice

½ teaspoon sea salt

½ cup fresh cilantro, chopped

Place the nuts, rejuvelac, and 1 teaspoon salt in a blender and process until smooth.

Place a strainer lined with cheesecloth over a bowl. Transfer the cheese mixture into the lined strainer, and twist the ends of the cheesecloth together and secure with a rubber band or twine. Place a plate on top of the wrapped cheese ball and add a weight on top, such as a mason jar filled with water, heavy enough to gently press the extra liquid out of the cheese. Cover the mixture with a clean kitchen towel and allow to culture for 24 to 48 hours at room temperature.

Transfer the cheese to a bowl and stir in the seasoning ingredients. Mix well with a flexible spatula. Line a container with plastic wrap or cheesecloth. Spoon the cheese into the container and pack it tightly. Cover and refrigerate for 6 to 8 hours to let firm and set.

Wrap the cheese in plastic wrap. Store in a sealed container in the refrigerator. Will keep, refrigerated, for 1 to 2 weeks.

AGED GRUYÈRE

This firm, smooth-textured cheese with a rustic rind gives way to an aromatic interior with a robust, assertive flavor. A superb cheese to enjoy with wine, fruit, and crackers as well as to add to your favorite sandwiches. To give this Gruyère its signature rind, you will need to use a dehydrator or the lowest setting on your oven.

Makes about 10 ounces

PREP AND COOK TIME
30 minutes

WAIT TIME
24 to 48 hours to culture, 8 to 12 hours to set and develop flavor, and 8 to 12 hours to create rind

Seed-Free / Soy-Free

CHEESE

2 cups raw, blanched almonds, soaked, rinsed, and drained (see page 28)

¾ cup rejuvelac (see page 38)

1 teaspoon sea salt

SEASONING

2 tablespoons nutritional yeast

2 tablespoons chickpea miso paste

Place all the cheese ingredients in a blender and process until smooth and creamy. Do not overprocess, as this can overheat the mixture and harm the culture.

Place a strainer lined with cheesecloth over a bowl. Transfer the cheese mixture into the lined strainer, and twist the ends of the cheesecloth together and secure with a rubber band or twine. Place a plate on top of the wrapped cheese ball and add a weight on top, such as a mason jar filled with water, heavy enough to gently press the extra liquid out of the cheese. Cover the mixture with a clean kitchen towel and allow to culture for 24 to 48 hours at room temperature.

Transfer the cheese to a bowl and stir in the seasoning ingredients. Mix well with a flexible spatula. Line a container with plastic wrap or cheesecloth. Spoon the cheese into the container and pack it tightly. Cover and refrigerate for 6 to 8 hours to firm and set.

After the cheese has set, create the rind: Remove the cheese from the container and place it in a dehydrator. Dehydrate for 8 to 12 hours at 115°F. Alternatively, you can use your oven on the lowest possible setting. The drying time will vary, depending on how much moisture is left in the fermented cheese.

Wrap the cheese in waxed paper. Store in a sealed container in the refrigerator. Will keep, refrigerated, for 1 to 2 weeks.

VARIATIONS AND SUBSTITUTIONS If you like a sharper-flavored cheese and do not have a dehydrator, you can try this variation for an air-dried Gruyère. To air dry, remove the cheese from the mold once it's firm, and rub salt evenly over the entire surface. Cover the cheese carefully with cheesecloth and place on a cooking rack in a cool place that has good air circulation. Let air dry for 2 to 3 days. The salt will protect and flavor the cheese.

CREAMY DANISH BLUE

————//————

This creamy blue variety is sharp and tangy with the characteristic blue-green veins that give blue cheese its name. A good drizzling of maple syrup will help bring out the flavor of this hearty cheese. Enjoy on lettuce wedges and crumbled on sliced tomatoes.

Makes 10 to 12 ounces

PREP AND COOK TIME
30 minutes

WAIT TIME
48 to 72 hours to culture and 48 to 72 hours to set and develop flavor

Seed-Free / Soy-Free

2 cups raw cashews, soaked, rinsed, and drained (see page 28)

½ cup organic refined coconut oil, melted

1 tablespoon chickpea miso paste

2 teaspoons sea salt

½ teaspoon onion powder

½ teaspoon garlic powder

½ cup rejuvelac (see page 38)

¼ teaspoon spirulina

Place all the ingredients, except the spirulina, in a blender and process until smooth.

Transfer the mixture to a container with a lid and let sit at room temperature to culture for a total of 48 to 72 hours. During the fermentation process, the mixture will develop air pockets, rise, and thicken. After 24 hours, smell and taste the cheese for desired sharpness.

After the culturing period, stir the cheese until creamy and dot the surface with the spirulina. Fold the cheese over a few times to create the blue-green veins.

Scoop and pack the cheese into a container lined with plastic wrap. Cover and refrigerate for another 48 to 72 hours to let the cheese ripen.

Wrap the cheese in plastic wrap. Store in a sealed container in the refrigerator. Will keep, refrigerated, for 1 to 2 weeks. The cheese will become firmer and the flavor will continue to develop as it ages.

Sea salt is made from evaporated sea water. With minimal processing, it is heavier in natural trace minerals than table salt.

DRUNKEN GOAT

———— // ————

A delightful chèvre-inspired cheese wrapped in brandy-cured Red Russian kale leaves. It is bursting with fragrant and indulgent flavors that turn creamy in your mouth. A perfect centerpiece for any special occasion. Serve with fruits and crusty bread.

Makes about 1 pound

PREP AND COOK TIME
30 minutes

WAIT TIME
48 hours to culture and 24 hours to set and develop flavor

Seed-Free / Soy-Free

CHEESE

1 cup raw hazelnuts, soaked, rinsed, and drained (see page 28)

1 cup raw cashews, soaked, rinsed, and drained (see page 28)

¾ cup rejuvelac (see page 38)

1 teaspoon sea salt

INFUSION

¼ cup organic brandy

4 to 6 organic Red Russian kale leaves

SEASONING

3 tablespoons nutritional yeast

1 tablespoon chickpea miso paste

Place all the cheese ingredients in a blender and process until smooth.

Place a strainer lined with cheesecloth over a bowl. Transfer the cheese mixture into the lined strainer, and twist the ends of the cheesecloth together and secure with a rubber band or twine. Place a plate on top of the wrapped cheese ball and add a weight on top, such as a mason jar filled with water, heavy enough to gently press the extra liquid out of the cheese. Cover the mixture with a clean kitchen towel and allow to culture for 48 hours at room temperature.

While the cheese ferments, wash and dry the kale leaves and place them in a glass container. Pour the brandy over the leaves, cover, and let soak and infuse for 48 hours at room temperature.

After fermentation is complete, unwrap the cheese and place it in a mixing bowl. Add the seasoning ingredients and mix to combine. Taste, and adjust to your liking.

Choose a container, keeping in mind that it will serve to shape your cheese, and line it with plastic

wrap. Pat the kale leaves dry, using a paper towel, and begin placing them in the lined container, making sure they overlap on all sides. Spoon the cheese into the center, pressing firmly to distribute evenly. Wrap the ends of the leaves inward to cover the cheese. Cover and let the cheese ripen in the refrigerator for a minimum of 24 hours.

Wrap the cheese in plastic wrap. Store in a sealed container in the refrigerator. Will keep, refrigerated, for 1 week.

CHEESE TRUFFLES

————————//————————

These sweet, single-serving cheese truffles are light, yet rich in flavor. Pair the colorful little globes with other cheeses, fruits, and crackers to create a stunning cheese platter.

Makes about 10 ounces

PREP AND COOK TIME
30 minutes

WAIT TIME
48 hours to culture and 6 to 8 hours to set and develop flavor

Seed-Free / Soy-Free

CHEESE

2 cups raw cashews, soaked, rinsed, and drained (see page 28)

½ cup rejuvelac (see page 38)

3 tablespoons nondairy, soy-free yogurt

½ teaspoon sea salt

SEASONING

2 tablespoons nutritional yeast

1 tablespoon fresh lemon juice

½ teaspoon pure vanilla extract

2 tablespoons pure maple syrup

COATING SUGGESTIONS

Dried apricots and rosemary

Rose hip flakes

Pistachios and golden berries

Place all the cheese ingredients in a blender. Process until smooth and creamy, occasionally stopping to scrape down the sides of the blender and move the mixture down toward the blades. Transfer to a glass container, cover, and let culture at room temperature for 48 hours.

When fermentation is complete, stir in the seasoning ingredients and blend well. Cover and refrigerate for 6 to 8 hours to allow the cheese to firm and set.

After the cheese has set, scoop up the cheese mixture 1 teaspoon at a time and roll into 1-inch balls. Roll them in the coating of your choice.

Store, refrigerated, in a sealed container; will keep for 1 to 2 weeks.

TRICK OF THE TRADE For dessert cheeses, allow the mixture to culture for a minimum of 48 hours. This will create the necessary tanginess that complements a sweeter cheese.

PAIRINGS AND ACCOMPANIMENTS

BUILDING THE PERFECT VEGAN CHEESE PLATE

ALTHOUGH CHEESE ITSELF IS A NEAR PERFECT SNACK, COMPLEMENTING it with crisp and chewy textures, salty and sweet flavors, and fresh and juicy contrasts can truly delight the senses.

Follow these simple rules to ensure a winning cheese plate every time:

- Select three to five cheeses, to avoid overwhelming your guests.
- Try to include a variety of textures and flavors, such as:

  SOFT: Camembert, Herbed Farmer Cheese, Triple Peppercorn

  HARD: Cheddar, Swiss, Aged Feta, Apple-Smoked Gouda

  BLUE: Gorgonzola, Danish Blue

  SWEET: Maple Fig Double Cream, Dark Chocolate Brie, Chai-Spiced

- Try the "opposites attract" rule: Pair a hard cheese with a soft baguette; a soft cheese with a crispy cracker; a salty cheese with a sweet jam or preserve; a dry cheese with a serving of juicy fruit.
- Set out a variety of sweet and savory tidbits to accompany your cheeses.

A SELECTION OF BREADS, including sliced baguette, bread sticks, and crackers in all different shapes and sizes. It's a good idea to vary taste and texture among the breads as well as the cheeses.

JARRED CONDIMENTS AND PICKLED VEGETABLES, sweet preserves, tart chutneys, and spicy mustards. You can also add artichoke hearts, cornichons, olives, and roasted red peppers.

VARIOUS OTHER SWEET AND SALTY ITEMS, caramelized pecans or spiced Marcona almonds, assorted seasonal and dried fruits, such as figs, cherries, apples, and pears.

VEGAN CHEESE PAIRINGS

WINE AND CHEESE PAIRINGS

Wine and cheese are two of life's great culinary pleasures, and finding the perfect match can be a delicious endeavor.

As with any food pairing, it helps to think of either complementary or contrasting flavors.

Fresh and soft cheeses, such as Ricotta (page 118), Mozzarella (page 105), Chèvre Noir (page 144), Herbed Feta (page 122), Brie (pages 96–98), and Camembert (page 108), love crisp whites, dry rosés, sparkling wines, dry aperitif wines, and light-bodied reds with low tannins. Avoid big, tannic red wines, such as Malbec, cabernet sauvignon, and Bordeaux. They will feel too astringent with the fresh cheeses.

Cheeses that have a firmer texture and stronger flavors, such as Dill Havarti (page 106), Golden Cheddar (page 102), or Cauliflower Jack (page 72), need medium-bodied whites, fruity reds, and aperitif wines that offer a balance between acidity, fruit, and tannin.

Blue cheeses, such as Gorgonzola (page 129), need wines with both boldness and sweetness to balance their flavors and savory body. Pair with ports, sauternes, and sherries.

Bold-flavored cheeses, such as Baked Feta (page 124), Aged Gruyère (page 160), or Mustard-Horseradish Encrusted Cheese (page 138) love full-bodied whites and tannic reds.

BEER AND CHEESE PAIRINGS

The outstanding range of beers available today makes beer pairing a versatile experience.

As with wines, choose beers with a similar intensity to your cheese—typically the more pungent the cheese, the more of a full character you want your beer to have. Then look for flavors that are either complementary or contrasting. Some cheeses show their best qualities when the beer is very different, whereas others stand out when paired with a beer that complements many of the same flavors.

Festive Two-Nut Cheese Balls (page 121) and Mozzarella (page 105) work well with the light, almost effervescent quality of most wheat beers.

The American Slices (page 71), Provolone (page 95), and Cauliflower Jack (page 72) match the intensity of moderately hoppy pilsners.

Golden Cheddar (page 102) and Habanero-Smoked Farmhouse Cheese (page 155) complement the robust flavors of brown ales.

The savory Gorgonzola (page 129) and Creamy Danish Blue (page 163) are a good match for the bold intensity of barley wines.

The nutty flavors of the Aged Gruyère (page 160) and the Swiss Cheese (page 76) play well against the maltiness of darker lagers.

Apple-Smoked Gouda (page 80) and the Smoked Chipotle (page 83) complement the moderately hoppy pale ales and amber ales.

The grassy, citrusy, fresh flavors of the Dill Havarti (page 106), Thai Spice Double Cream (page 158), and the Boursin-Style Garlic and Herb (page 117), play well with the citrus bitterness and fruity maltiness of an India Pale Ale (IPA).

The Mascarpone (page 149), the Ricotta (page 118), or the Sweet Spread (page 45) are a perfect match for fruit beers.

As with any pairing, think of either complementary
or contrasting flavors. Try tasting the cheese first
by itself, to get a sense of its character, and then
try another bite with your beverage of choice to see
how they mingle.

SPIRIT AND CHEESE PAIRINGS

Finally, if you're in the spirit of things, you're in luck. Most spirits lend themselves exceptionally well to cheese.

Try pairing the Pesto Ricotta (page 113), the Herbed Farmer Cheese (page 114), or Boursin-Style Garlic and Herb (page 117) with vodka. The clean spirit appreciates nuanced cheeses that help bring out the subtleties of its flavor. Pair with a light cocktail with fresh garden ingredients that will most complement the cheeses, such as a Lemon-Thyme Spritz, or a Cucumber Fizz.

Try a Triple Peppercorn Cheese (page 131), a Dill Havarti (page 106), or the aromatic Herbes de Provence Cheese (page 143) with gin. With its citrus and botanical notes, gin plays well with fresh, soft cheeses. Once again, keep your cocktails fresh and simple. Try a fresh citrus gimlet or the honey-sweetened Bees Knees.

The Chai-Spiced Cheese (page 84), the Dark Chocolate Brie (page 98), or the Maple-Fig Double Cream (page 147) pair delightfully with a quality sipping rum. With their subtle flavors of sweetness and complex notes ranging from smoky oak, vanilla, citrus, cocoa, and warming spices, quality rums will bring out the sweet, warming notes in dessert cheeses.

Smoky, meaty cheeses, such as the Baked Feta (page 124), Aged Gruyère (page 160), and Golden Cheddar (page 102), are a good match for peaty, spicy whiskies. The rich and nutty varieties, such as the Apple-Smoked Gouda (page 80), the nutty "Open Sesame" Cheese (page 66), or the Smoked Vegetable Cheese (page 69), pair better with more balanced blends and less smoky whiskeys. Try a rich, woodsy Manhattan or sip it straight.

Finally, when pairing with the complex range of tequilas, choose to pair milder, soft cheeses full of flavor, such as the Olive and Sun-Dried Tomato cheese (page 141) or the Arugula Pesto Cheese (page 92) with the crisp, citrusy, and floral notes of a blanco tequila. Try it on the rocks with a generous squeeze of fresh lime. The spiced Smoked Chipotle (page 83), or the savory Olive and Roasted Pepper Cheese Terrine (page 136) will work well with the equally spiced reposado tequila. Typically aged in oak barrels, this tequila takes on the oaky, smoky flavor unique to each distillery. Try it with a large ice cube and an orange twist. The bold, savory Danish Blue (page 163) or the Habanero-Smoked Farmhouse Cheese (page 155) will pair nicely with an añejo tequila. The full-bodied, smoky tequila is best sipped from a small brandy snifter.

ACKNOWLEDGMENTS

I'd like to think of this book as one delicious recipe bursting with fresh, juicy ingredients blended together to create a most delightful experience. It took a lot of masterful folks to produce the beautiful book you're holding right now.

This book would not be possible without my mom's culinary genius. She meticulously tested and retested every single recipe in this book. It has meant the world to me to work side-by-side with her on this project. I am forever grateful.

My dad deserves an honorable mention for giving up my mom to me for long stretches of time. He is also a creative force in the kitchen and undoubtedly passed some of his creative culinary juices on to me.

To my literary agent, Marilyn Allen, who has been there every step of the way of this exciting endeavor. Thank you, Marilyn, for believing in me. Your warmth and ongoing guidance is much appreciated.

To my editor extraordinaire, Ann Treistman, for brilliantly guiding me through this project. Your sharp and unwavering style is everything and I am most thankful.

To the entire Countryman Press team for the heaping spoonful of awesomeness poured into this book. Devorah Backman, for your savvy marketing talents; Aurora Bell, for your unwavering grace and support; Iris Bass, for your thorough and capable care of my words; to the design and production rockstars Devon Zahn, Nick Caruso, and Jessica Murphy. I am beyond grateful to work with all of your incredible talents.

A great big thank you to Gyorgy Papp for making the pages come alive with his beautiful photographs. Thank you for bringing my creative vision to life.

And to my dear friends, for sharing a million meals, a million adventures, a million laughs, a million failures, and a million successes. Here's to a million more! Thank you for your amazing presence in my life. You are forever loved.

RESOURCE GUIDE

INGREDIENTS

AMAZON.COM
A good source for agar, carrageenan, xanthan gum, and just about any other nonperishable ingredient you can't find locally, including a wide variety of nuts and seeds, both conventional and organic, at better prices than most other online purveyors

BARRYFARM.COM
Agar powder and xanthan gum

BULKFOODS.COM
Agar, xanthan gum, tapioca flour, arrowroot powder, and many other natural foods, including conventionally grown nuts and seeds, available in bulk

CRAFTBEERKINGS.COM
Online craft beer shop

DRINKUPNY.COM
Online spirits shop

FRUITSSTAR.COM
Offers nuts and seeds, both conventional and organic, in 1-pound and often 5-pound packages

GARAGISTE.COM
Online wine shop

IHERB.COM
Agar powder and xanthan gum

IGOURMET.COM
Gourmet pantry staples and condiments

LEPICERIE.COM
Agar, carrageenan, xanthan gum, and other hard-to-find ingredients, and also high-quality chocolate, flavoring extracts, exotic condiments and spices, and more

MODERNISTPANTRY.COM
A good source for carrageenan in reasonable quantities

MOUNTAINROSEHERBS.COM
All-natural organic spices, blends, dried herbs, edible flowers, and culinary salts

REDSTARYEAST.COM
Nutritional yeast

SOMMPICKS.COM
Online wine shop

VEGANESSENTIALS.COM
Vegan foods such as Lieber's vegan gelatin, coconut oils, and vegan milks and yogurts

VITACOST.COM
A wide selection of coconut oil, including Spectrum organic refined coconut oil

WILDERNESSFAMILYNATURALS.COM
Offers "organic, ultraclean, supreme expeller-pressed" coconut oil, which doesn't have a strong coconut flavor

KITCHEN TOOLS

BREVILLEUSA.COM
High-quality kitchen equipment, including high-speed blenders and food processors

CHEFSRESOURCE.COM
Kitchen tools and supplies, including pots, bowls, fine-mesh strainers, thermometers, and measuring cups

OXO.COM
Stainless-steel mesh strainers, citrus squeezers, and other kitchen gadgets

VITAMIX.COM
Premium high-speed blenders

WILLIAMS-SONOMA.COM
Pots, fine-mesh strainers, spoons, thermometers, and measuring cups

INDEX

//

*italics indicate illustrations

ABOUT THE AUTHOR

———————————— // ————————————

JULES ARON is a best-selling author, holistic health and wellness coach, and green life-style expert. She is deeply passionate about a healthy, wholesome lifestyle that includes delicious, nutritious foods that fuel the body, mind, and spirit. Aron holds a Masters degree from New York University, is a Certified Yoga Instructor, a Certified Qigong and Traditional Chinese Medicine Practitioner, and a Certified Health and Nutrition Coach from The Institute of Integrative Nutrition. She has been featured in the *New York Post*, *The Today Show*, *Well + Good NYC*, and *Mind Body Green*, as well as other national fitness and wellness magazines and websites, sharing with thousands the secrets to obtaining optimal health, both inside and out. Aron's first book, *Zen and Tonic: Savory and Fresh Cocktails for the Enlightened Drinker* is a best-selling cocktail book written for the health-conscious drinker.

Working with clients in her coaching practice, Aron found that the hardest thing for people to give up when embarking on a healthy lifestyle is, without a doubt, cheese. The primary protein in milk and cheese is casein. When the human body digests casein, it produces casomorphins, which have an opiate-like effect on humans. Because cheese is denser than milk, the casein is more heavily concentrated, which can explain the addictive effect we seem to experience. With her clients' struggle in mind, Aron created vegan cheese recipes made with wholesome plant-based ingredients, taking into account soy, nut, and seed allergies. The result is a fun, simple, and delicious recipe book for all to indulge in.

ABOUT THE PHOTOGRAPHER

GYORGY PAPP is a commercial photographer specializing in the culinary world. The Hungarian-born artist spent the first part of his life traveling the world before moving to Florida with his family. He is an espresso addict, a pastry chef, and a mixologist who enjoys exploring new places and making his sons smile. www.papphoto.com